MODERN TIMES AND HARD RHYMES

By
Laura J. Booker

All art and illustrations by K.T. Gore

Table of Contents

A WORD FROM THE AUTHOR

I started to pen my little odes during the first Covid lockdown, working from home with little else to do it gave me something creative to do, something I hadn't done for many years. I started to share my efforts on Twitter and quickly found others enjoyed them too and looked forward to my daily dose of, well...twaddle.
Twitter is an interesting place, sometimes fun, sometimes nasty, sometimes just plain weird, but it never ceases to entertain me or provide inspiration for my little rhymes.
People told me to capture these in a book, so here it is. I hope you enjoy them and the ones that made me type this lot up had better bloody buy a copy!

PS. Just remember to read them in a Yorkshire accent.

ACKNOWLEDGEMENTS

Thank you to everyone who made this book possible, my family for being there and making me weird but also keeping me sane, and to all the followers that told me to do this. Special mentions for James Tringham who encouraged me to pick up a pen and write and Peter Murphy my gimp gone rogue whose warped mind constantly provides inspiration, and everyone else whose kind words and encouragement made me get off my arse and do something. Thank you all so much.

INVISIBLE

I have a little secret
One I am going to share
One day what I was about 40
I simply wasn't there
Somehow I turned invisible
No longer could be seen
Men would look right through me
And shop girls were just mean
The doors would swing back in my face
In shops I was ignored
When people finally noticed me
They'd act like they were bored
In queues people barge past me
At bars I'd dehydrate
My powers of invisibility
Simply were too great
I wish that I'd been warned of this
So that I could get a sign
That says "oi bitch
You serve me first
And you lot get in line"
I may be knocking on a bit
I might not be in my youth
But I've something I want to share with you
Here's a painful truth
One day you'll be transparent too
And people will not see
So let us hope when that day comes
You're not waiting in front of me

BRAS

Why do bras hate me?
Can someone tell me that?
I push my boobs in round the front
They pop out round the back
I'm sure I line my jugs up, at the start of every day
But by lunchtime I've got one up here
And the others run away
The straps dig in, the wires pop out
It's such a blooming hassle
I can't even start to think
How you wear a nipple tassel!
At the airport you can guarantee
I'll set off the alarms
I'm sick of having to show the staff
My more than ample charms
All the really sexy stuff is made
For the girls all slim and trim
For girls like me with more to see
We need more…scaffolding
Oh why do bras hate me?
I say this every day
I'll stay a mess
I'll wear a vest
And throw the chuffs away

RE-USE

I've been green instead of buying new
I will reuse
which means I found new ways to feed
my habit of buying bags and shoes.
I've been on eBay Gumtree tried the lot
there's real bargains to be had
and it's so cheap you can get twice as much
not to do it would be mad.
There's no need to hit the cheap shops
for stuff that just lasts a short while
pay just the same and get quality
that won't go out of style.
Why not benefit from those folk
that wear things once then throw away
you can't beat that feeling of a bargain
it really makes your day.
I know I'm tight and I'm from Yorkshire
but nothing feels so good to me
as paying a fiver for a designer coat
that's BNWT
Now I wouldn't get everything on there
Some things are a bit strange
I mean some people are selling undies
I would be scared that I'd get mange!
My greatest purchase ever
the one with which I have great pride
is the five pound Biba bag
that had a tenner zipped inside.
But I'm serious just have a look
stop the disposable culture
but watch out if you're bidding against me
cause I'm in there like a vulture!

GAMBLING

I've seen them ads for online gambling
so I thought I'd have a go
but when I got logged in
there was so much I didn't know.
I remember as a kid
my grandad hung out at the bookies
and came back home with a face
like someone had kicked him in the chuckies.
We all knew secretly
that at times he did quite well
but he kept it hidden from my grandma
and so, we didn't tell.
With him I understood it
just to win or each way bets
but now there's BUR and BIP and accies
and other stuff that I forget.
It's like a different language
and way too complicated for me
I just wanted to put a fiver on to win
on a big 'oss at Aintree.
So, I went down to the bookies
to ask for a hot tip
but there were some funny sorts in there
I really didn't dare let slip,
that I didn't get the lingo
going dutching with a Trixie
I don't even know her
but it made me worried and a bit twitchy.
So, I settled for the bingo
much simpler than them other things
I'm all set up with me dobber
and I've got them bingo wings.

RECYCLE

I've been trying to recycle
got the colour coded bins
I've been washing and categorising
and remembering which to put them in.
I know it's for the greater good
and it makes me feel a good lass
but once a week all the neighbours can see
why I've got such a fat ass!
the pizza boxes piled high
the bottles go clinky clinky
I don't think it's a secret now
that I like a little drinky.
I wish there was some way
I could discreetly hide
all the evidence of junk food
we have tried to sneak outside.
But at least I'm not as bad
as the ones that live next door to me
judging by what they put out
they've got a short life expectancy.
With the tinnies and the processed food
is a wonder they're still alive
the bin men had to make two trips
to get it off their drive!
But seriously folks let's keep it up
lets recycle everything
I'm putting out my other half
if someone wants to take him in.

CATS

Cats are sadists, yes its true
No one will tell you that
No one is more perverted
Thank the cute and fluffy cat
Forget about your Mr Grey
Your nipple clamps and straps
Your cat just wants to torture you
Humiliated by your cats
Not only will they hurt you
Bite you, scratch you, even more
They make you beg for their affections
Like a thirsty little whore
At dinner time they'll flirt with you
Give kisses and the like
But as soon as they have had their treats
They'll snub you
On your bike!
They test you, try to injure you to see what you can stand
Like trip you on the stairs
Or stick their hook claws in your hand
They wait till you've got visitors
When you're showing them 'how cute'
Then they stop with their affections
Bite you, then give you the boot
So why do I put up with them?
There's no benefits I can see
I suppose its cos deep down I know
They're really just like me
So come here my little sadist
Let us start a little gang
I'll kit out the dungeon
You go find me a hot man!

DICK PICS

Oh not another dick pic!
It's getting very silly
I'm going to cry if I have to spy
One more shrivelled up willy!
It's getting awfully tiresome
You showing me your wares
You could have at least washed your hands
And trimmed those pubic hairs
Please don't be offended
Don't let this come between us
Its just that I'm not really
Attracted to your penis
I don't want to 'chat' or 'play'
So I don't need to see your face
The fact that you just flashed me
Is frankly a disgrace
That's right you are a flasher!
Not that there's anything much to flash
I think you'll have better luck elsewhere
If you spend a little cash
I'm sure the lovely ladies
On Only Fans or the like
Would love to see your todger
But not me, I'm not a bike
I'm not sorry we have to part now
Your words aren't soft and tender
You're cheap and tacky matey
So go do one with your member
So here's a plea from all us ladies
Before you send us all your cock
All that you'll be getting
Is a big report and block

FREE TO A GOOD HOME

Does anyone want to run off with me
And start another life
My current state
Is not that great
But I'll mek a decent wife
I'm sort of, almost tidy
I clean up after missen
I tek no looking after
And I'm fast asleep by ten
I'm quite a happy little sausage
I don't like doom and gloom
And as I'm only 5 foot 2
I don't take up that much room
My cooking skills are middling
Just trust me and you'll see
But if I accidentally poison you
I'll take you straight to A & E
I think you'll find me lovely
I don't whinge and I don't nag
And in matters of the bedroom
I'm a complete and utter…angel

SHOWERS

Showers are not self-cleaning
They get covered in soap scum
That bounces off your bits
When you are soaping up your bum
So do us all a favour
And give the shower a clean
We don't want your bum bits
We don't know where you've been
And while we're in the shower
Fight the urge to have a pee
If I'm coming in straight after you
I don't want that on me
And if you take off the shower head
And put it somewhere new
Please wipe and put it back again
But don't tell me what you do
If there's any other shower fun
You get up to on your own
Please don't make a little film
Or send it on your phone
Cos rest assured
Before you give the old chap such an outing
We won't be looking at your junk
Just checking out your mucky grouting

A YORKSHIRE PUDDING

I'm going to attempt to write
A ditty short and sweet
To help me speak correctly
So you can understand my tweets
I know sometimes I may slip in
A little Yorkshire twang
But that is only for effect
This is really how I am
I say my aitches where required
And drop the extra tees
Ah come on you know its bollocks
I'm common as muck me

A WORLD FULL OF WAZZOCKS

The world is full of wazzocks
They're everywhere I go
And I'm sure you will be nodding
Cos just like me you just know
The ones that stop-start with their trollies
When perusing all the food
Reading all the blooming labels
Oh, it really is too rude
I'll bet they're the same pillocks
Who will park right at the side
Of me, leaving just a teeny gap
As though I'm one inch wide
Believe all they see in the papers
And the politicians' hype
If they said so then it must be true
They swallow any load of tripe
They think soap operas are real
And people care about their life
When they're standing outside Lidl
Shouting and bawling at their wife
Or swinging their screechy children
By their legs into the trolley
If it were up to me
There'd be penalties
For being such a wally
But the biggest of offenders
Whose crimes really are the worst
Are the ones when making cups of tea
Put the bloody milk in first!

HOLES

Holes consume the internet
They're everywhere you go
You can't scroll for 5 minutes
Without seeing someone's down below
Which led me onto thinking
Why the fascination with these gaps
I'd rather pass the day
Without a star fish or your flaps
I'm sure people are queuing up
To see them in their legions
But call me a prude
I think its rude
To post your nether regions
I mean there are some holes
I don't even want
My own doctor to see
Well maybe apart from that new fit one
But he's much too young for me
Between jiggling boobs and twerking buns
And things thrust in between
There's some creative uses for them holes
Based on the things I've seen
There's oils and lubes and other things
Looks like some creamy sort of stuff
That they moisten their many holes with
They must suffer from dry chuff
So call me a stiff or failure
But I think I'm going to pass
I don't want your genitalia
Or to look right up your ass

PRIME DELIVERY

I don't know about the rest of you
But the best relationship in my life
Is with a certain delivery guy
Who sees me more than his wife
It's not that I am lazy
Well ok, maybe a bit
But its so easy to add to basket
That do that real life shopping shit
A nice little subscription
Means I never need to leave
The comfort of my own abode
Not when I've got Steve
I think that is his proper name
That's what it said on his love letter
I'm sorry you're not in he said
Look in the bin for your new sweater
He likes to leave me little gifts
But never asks for hugs
Sometimes he leaves my parcels in the soil
Where they're adorned with snails and slugs
I've tried to show affection
But he's like lightning on his feet
He's up and off away again
Before I'm out my seat
I don't think that there's a future though
For me and driver dude
If he keeps on running away
We'll never get to get rude
I think I'll shift affection
To the bloke from DPD
He's a bit slower off the mark
As he's got a dodgy knee!

CARBS

This is a love letter
To the thing I hold most dear
And I think you'll be surprised to know
Its not chocolate gin or beer
Its carbs I love with all my heart
That full up sense of stodge
From eating half a loaf of bread
Then feeling sick and podged
It think it's an addiction
I have no self control
When it comes to choosing sex or carbs
I'll go for the bread roll
On Friday the anticipation
Of that pizza and those fries
You'll never witness that much love
EVER in my eyes
If I were a man I'm sure that it'd give me a proper boner
But I'll not complain
I'll get my kicks
From that full on carby coma
That toast smothered in melted butter
A jacket tatey full of cheese
The carby dense deliciousness
That brings me to my knees
I know my body suffers
I have excess insulation
But carb frenzies keep me safe from harm
I'll never suffer from starvation
So how much do I love these carbs
The stottie, roll or bap
Well enough to say
Stop insulting them
By calling them such crap
There's just one think I need to clarify
A point I really have to make
When referring to the think I love
We call it a bread cake!!

TROUBLE IN STORE

Those of you that know me
Will know how much I deplore
Going to the supermarket
It really is a bore
The creepy secret touchers
That push against you at the till
If you get any closer mate
I'll have to go back on the pill
Or the intense bargain hunters
That seek out yellow labels
They'll take your bloody eye out
For those 10 pence fruity bagels
I try to avoid all people
So I'll go through the self serve
Its my way of not having to speak
And keeps your distance from the pervs
But for some reason when I'm stood there
Under the red flashing light
Waiting for authorisation
Like some lady of the night
The staff choose to ignore me
And serve everyone else instead
Its not like I'm stood glaring
Like I want to punch them in the head
But its not just all the people
That get right on my tits
Its things like charging 50p
For a bag for all my bits
Exploiting all us greedy folk
Trying to carry more than we're able
I wouldn't get so much
If it weren't for those bloody 10p bagels!

BACK SEAT DRIVER

Sometimes when I'm out driving
Someone else will come along
And their fantastic at just pointing out
The things they think I do wrong
What gear are you in? they ask
I mean who honestly watches that?
The one that doesn't burn the engine out
You condescending twat!
They accuse me of being aggressive
Then harass me to overtake
While I think of giving them whiplash
Like if I suddenly were to brake
You drive too fast
You drive too slow
Why are you parking over here?
Your windscreen wipers are on too fast
Yes, I hear you dear!
Maybe if you want to contribute
Go play with the petrol pump
It costs me so much extra
Dragging round a useless lump
My car gets picked on too
Why all the girly stuff and bling?
Well you see if its too glitzy for you

Simply don't get in
I'll drive around in peace
Singing along to mamma mia
You stay at home and fiddle on your phone
Or go and watch top gear
And just to say my licence has never had
A single point in sight
Remind me how many did you get
When you ran through that red light?
Yes backseat drivers are the worst
They kick up such a fuss
So if you going to diss my driving mate
Please go and get the bus

MUMS

For all you potential mums to be
I'll tell you how it is

So you have a chance to change your mind
Of how to use that jizz
Don't be silly pregnancy's beautiful
I hear you cry and holler
Well once you've heard my tales of woe
You might just decide to swallow
From the moment you conceive
Your body starts to change and how
So say goodbye to all you pert firm bits
They're all past history now
Morning sickness it will wake you up
And wake you in the night
You can also spew
In the workplace too
And permanently look like shite
You've piles and all the stitches too
To face after you've sprogged
You'll pray that your insides don't fall out
When you're sitting on the bog
Your tits are huge and sore and bruised
You think that if you cough
You'll pee yourself and possibly
Your nipples will fall off
Maternity clothes are comfy though
I will give you that
But not really worth the price
Of ripping open your twat
All your self respect is gone
Who'd have ever thought before
You'd let rip with a roomful watching
As you poo upon the floor
And all the breathing exercises
Won't counteract that twinge
As you push that HUGE bundle of joy
Out of your tiny minge
So I hear you ask, is it worth it though?
Will the bad memories soon be gone?
Well let's say family planning wise
I stopped after the one

GLAMOUR PUSS

I wish I was a glamour puss
Like all the other girls
With the long sleek hair and savoir faire
Instead I've got these curls
I'm sure way back in my family tree
Someone cross bred with a lion
Cos I got stuck with this here mane
That I can't even iron
I think that I've had stunted growth
A defective gene or two
See those sex machines all tall and lean
Yet I'm fat and five foot 2
I try my best I really do
To cover up the grey
But without a second mortgage
There's some bits won't go away
I'll go adapt my hoover
And I'll try and do home liposuction
But what to do with all that goo
From my DIY breast reduction
I get the ads for panties
In my insta feed each day
You know the ones up to your neck
Where you squash that fat away
It seems a bit uncomfy
Your whole body in you knicks
Surely you just end up with your belly
Squeezed up like extra tits
So I've given up
I'll never be
A glamour puss like them
I'll just sit here in my muu muu
A solid 2 ½ out of 10

JUNK FOOD ADS

I would like to make a formal complaint
about those junk food ads
cos what I see on the telly
looks nowt like what I've had.
Big succulent burgers
with salad piled up high
mine's all tiny and looks sat on
I think they might have lied.
Where's my juicy tomatoes?
and gently toasted buns?
and my mayo's a bit runny
looks like someone's been having fun!
I've a box of sweaty chicken
it's got saggier thighs than me
and whoever tossed my salad
is indeed a tosser it's clear to see.
On the ads the customers are happy
but they are all actors of course
in real life we are all saddened by
the absence of barbecue sauce.
It's not just the food they lie about
it's the happy smiling staff
that listen to your order

then mess it up for a laugh.
Enjoy your meal they tell me
as I slowly drive away
and pull up round the corner
to see what they forgot today.
No sauce or no gravy?
I don't like dry nuggets you twat
the only moisture in this meal
is off the layer of fat.
I'd try to wash it down
with a delicious milkshake, that's the cure
but unlike the one on telly
mine is solid and won't come up the straw.
So, stop teasing us with your stunt food
we all know it's got a body double
just give us what you advertised
or there's gonna be trouble.

TOILETS

I have a toilet complex
That I'd like to share with you
Its not just an excuse to make
Cheap jokes about wee and poo
You see its not that I'm a clean freak
I just don't like others mess
So when I'm caught short out in public
This can cause me great distress
If there's any trace of substance
On the seat, paper, wall or floor
Then I simply can't be seated
And I'll start backing out the door
Yes I'm one of those strange people
That keeps cocking up the queue
Popping in and out the cubicles
In the search for a clean loo
Hurry up you freak
I hear them cry
You're causing a lot of bother
So then I have to hold my breath
And grit my teeth while I just hover
By now I really just can't pee

So I just pretend I've gone
Then come back in a little while
When the queue isn't as long
Or best of all just hold it in
And ignore the stomach cramps
A bit of mild kidney failure
Better than loos occupied by tramps
As well as all the nasty germs
There's secret listeners too
That seem to take forever
When you're dying for a poo
Just go away
So I can drop the kids off at the pool
Only deviants will wait around
We all know this is the rule
But they faff about
Doing their hair
While you're working up a sweat
Trying to hold inside that doo doo
With all the force of an Exocet
So please my toilet buddies
Make it nicer for us all
Wipe the seat down when you've finished
And bugger off out of the stall

WILLIES

Why are men obsessed with willies
And telling, no showing us its size
There's a lot more women value
Than what sits between your thighs
And for girls that tell you different
Well they're probably having you on
You'll be a source of mirth
As she compliments the girth
And length of your precious schlong
And for some reason men always touch them
Or rearrange their bits
I'm sure you wouldn't like it
if I did that with my tits
your todger if I'm honest
ain't the prettiest of things
and that goes for his supporters
you know, your saggy ball bearings
I know some fellas do try harder
And manscape the willy zone
But some just let it grow wild
And then wonder why we moan
You know try a bit of soap and water
If you really want to please
Cos I'm not particularly fond of
Any hint of well…knob cheese
And please stop taking those photos
No matter how proud of your erection
You'll make us want to go veggie
And stop shopping in the sausage section
So I've said my bit, just keep it in your pants
All clean and neat
Cost you've more chance of getting it looked at
If you're respectful clean and sweet

WEAR A MASK

Wear a mask you naughty people
Keep your nasty germs insider
It's not an inconvenience
And the plus point is it hides
All the scary people's faces
You know some things are best unseen
And while you're at it wash your hands again
Let's keep those fingers clean
I've lost count of all the people
I've had to subtly remind
That a mask under the nose
Is as good as one on your behind
I reckon those that don't comply
Should be turned away from shops
Or made to wear a diver's helmet
That should catch their nasty drops
I know some complain they're sweaty
Or they steam up behind their glasses
Buts its better than the rona
So come on you lads and lasses
Just take one for the team
And stick that mask upon your face
Its not about just you
You're helping all the human race

SHOP GIRL

Shop girl why do you hate me?
When I walk into your shop
And why is when I ask for help
You virtually throw a strop?
Is my presence an inconvenience?
Do you have grander things to do
Than serve your paying customers
And look at them like poo?
I must say your snooty expression
Isn't very well, inviting
Its not my fault your career choice
Isn't something more exciting
I work hard to earn my wages
To spend them on things that I desire
But your sour face deters me
And repels your potential buyer
I'd rather eat ground glass
Than add commission to your wages
For someone who simply just ignores me
Then leaves me waiting round for ages
I suggest a new career
One where ideally you work alone
Or one where we can't see you
Like working on a telephone
Where you can pull those moody faces
And no one else has to endure
You can sulk away in silence
Your bad attitude obscured
And just remember dearie
When you ready for a change
Don't apply to work for me
You see life it can be strange
I may not be keen to interview
When in your work history I start to delve
As I remember that look you gave me
When I asked if you had this in a twelve

15 MINUTES OF FAME

They reckon everyone has their moment
their 15 minutes of fame
but what happens if it came and I missed it
do I get to go again?
I suppose I don't want to be famous
infamous is more my thing
It's more likely as I don't have
any actual skills to bring.
Some people seek the limelight
they'll do owt on TV
but they all seem a bit desperate
and not a normal sort like me.
I suppose it would be okay to know
you did something interesting in your life
but not the sort of interesting
that gets you on Channel 5.
To be honest 15 minutes feels quite demanding
I know I was here and I'm alive
I don't really want the hassle
Can I settle for just five?
In fact give my 15 minutes
to someone else
I'm sure I'm way too shy
I wouldn't know just what to say
if I was in the public eye.
There's plenty others will take it
super keen to be a star
I'll write about them in my poems
and comment from afar.
Let the others have the glory
for my poems they can be my muse
cos the only programme I'll get on
is Crimewatch or the news.

HUSBANDS

Husbands, do we have to?
They're a real pain in the butt
They just sit there watching telly
With the odd grumble whinge and tut
They never do their little jobs
Not without 6 months of pleading
Just to put up a few pictures
Or when the radiators need bleeding
Yet my to do list is extensive
He will add new things each day
And then when I try to do them
He keeps getting in the way
I'm particularly fond of the daily question
You know…what's for tea?
I've no idea darling
Where are you taking me?
They dominate the telly
They won't let go of the remote
Its as though equality never happened
Are you sure I can still vote?
Any poo and sick related tasks
I think you'll find are mine
I'm also the only one that knows
How to operate a washing line
And don't start me on the aromas
He seems to generate
I'm sure he didn't smell like that
When we first started to date
I think I'd like a new one
Cos I reckon mines gone off
Preferably one that doesn't burp, fart, scratch or cough
So husbands, do we have to?
He's the bane of my life
I think that I'd be better off
If I go and find a wife

WHEN LOCKDOWN ENDS

When lockdown ends, I'm going out
To where, I don't quite know
But I'm sure it'll take some hours
Before I'm prepped and ready to go
There's a lot to be addressed
Before I'm stepping out the door
My crazy hair and the bits down there
Hairy legs and maybe more
They'd better clean the drains out
After I've finished my depilating
There'll be queues in every bathroom
With our fellas impatiently waiting
How much longer are you going to be?
I want to shave my beard
We'll be saying to our husbands
It's bigger than yours I fear
And choosing the perfect outfit
Well that really could take some time
I've had 12 months of buying
Outfits I can't wear yet online
I'll have forgotten how to walk in heels
I'll have to start wearing a bra
And non-elasticated waistbands
Are my biggest fear so far
There's one good thing though, one thing I know
I've really learned how to queue
That Morrisons pre training
For waiting at the bar for an hour or two
But wherever I end up going
I'll look fabulous without a doubt
For I'll have spent an entire year
Getting ready to go out

CATFISH

I think I'll become a catfish
And steal everybody's loot
I don't quite know how to do it
But it sounds like quite a hoot
You see someone stole my photo
And stuck it on a dating site
With intent to fleece some nice guys
But they can't be doing it right
You see they can't be very good at it
Or they'd pick someone young and pretty
Unless they're looking for some kind soul
Wants to help me out of pity
I've heard of overseas or military types
You know the blokes with tragic lives
You know the recently bereaved ones
In need of future mums and wives
I'll have to create a fake persona
One a bit less weird than me
That fellas will fall in love with
And want to send their cash to me
I reckon I'll need someone else's photo
To draw them in as bait
As my own fair reflection
Hasn't worked that well for me to date
In fact my own personal situation
While grim it isn't tragic
I'll need some form of ailment
Or horror to work that magic
You know it feels like too much effort
This whole catfish stuff takes time
I think I'll stay skint and honest
And keep writing these rubbish rhymes

THONGS

Thongs are wrong in many ways
And these I will outline
Its never right to stick up your arse
Something thinner than a washing line
They ride up high and go in deep
Much further than they ought to
In my mind your undies never should
Be making your eyes water
That funny pose you have to strike
When performing an extraction
I can't say it's a sexy look
I just don't see the attraction
If I wanted to hurt myself this way
In a bid to feel that twinge
I could just wear an elastic band
And pull it up my minge
In winter they are rubbish
Leaving your cheeks chapped and exposed
You really want something sensible
On your bum under your clothes
In summer its unhygienic
Just a sweaty bit of string
That'll just divide and chafe you
And we all know where that's been
I know some people find them sexy
But I'm here to tell you no!
Leaving things to your imagination
Is much sexier and so
I shall always avoid the evil thong
And I'll reassure you that
You never see, cheese wire up me
Dissecting my bum crack

HATERS

For some reason people hate me
And take any chance to have a dig
I've been called some lovely things
Like ugly thick whore and stupid pig
Yet no one knows me really
So I don't know why these people hate

But I've had this since I was a child
Getting bullied outside school gates
Back then it was for being clever
Or sticking up for my mates
I though this would stop as I got older
But looks like it never abates
If you knew me you'd know
How hard I try
To be upbeat bright and cheery
And look after the ones I love
No matter how tired or weary
But constant little digs and knocks
Each day chip away some more
Try to bring me down and dim my light
So I'll be darker than before
But I'll tell you this you haters
I may have been beaten down and cried
But I'll never be as twisted
As what you have got inside
If you need to hurt nice people
For a small and fleeting high
You're a weak and shallow person
So maybe ask yourself just why?
What's missing in your life to make
You vindictive cruel and small?
Do you crave negative attention
Just so you can walk tall?
With your over inflated ego
You bully, belittle and try to hurt
But I've a bigger heart that you'll ever have
So just crawl back down in the dirt
Because I am going nowhere
And I have friends here by my side
I'll always show my feelings
Because I have nothing to hide
That's cos I'm a real person
I wear my heart upon my sleeve
Unlike you, well no one likes you
So I think that you should leave

SPIDER

There's a spider in my bathtub
And it's really awfully near
I know I should just go and extract it
But I'm petrified with fear
If I move even the slightest bit
I'm sure that he'll attack
And if I panic and lose sight of him
He could end up down my back
People say its more scared of you
Than you are scared of it
But I'm not buying any of that
It looks an evil little shit
We've been staring each other now
For half and hour or so
I haven't moved from this here spot
Cos I'm not sure which way he'll go
My phobias quite a bad one
I'd go so far as to say
I'm considering burning the house down
Just to make him go away
Someone needs to get the hoover
So I can suck him up the hose

I'd go myself but if I turn my back
I know he'll go in my clothes
So I'm stood here completely naked
Except my slippers and my pants
Considering self defence moves
In case he chooses to advance
Maybe I could freeze him with the hairspray
Or trap him in a beaker
There must be some cleaning product in here
That at least will make him weaker
But maybe it'll give him super powers
Increase his spidey senses
He'll take over the entire street
Eating pets and smashing fences
Ok that might be a bit dramatic
I may be a little carried away
I'll just turn the tap on nice and fast
And flush that pest away

TABLETS

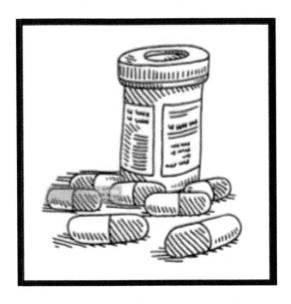

I'm kept alive by tablets
Some for this that and the other
But if you think that I take a lot
You should see my mother
How old people just keep track of them
It's a mystery to me
With a little box for everyday
You need a meds degree
Some they take first in the morning
With just a morning drink
Then others before and after meals
They really have to think
Some mean you can't eat grapefruit
Now what's that all about?
Good job none stop you eating cake
Well except the ones for gout
My parents are so full of pills
You would think that they would make
A lovely little rattling noise

If I were to give them a shake
My mum's knowledge of pharmaceuticals
Is extensive, really its mad
They'll be making a programme about her
Over 70s breaking bad
They'll be knocking out the good shit
To all the kids with no restrictions
A little cottage industry
Funded by their free prescriptions
So if you want to cure anything
Need a solution for all your ills
Just go and see my mum
I'm sure she'll have some super pills

UNDIES

Some people wear posh undies
All that sexy lingerie
But there's a secret hidden problem
Well, with what mine does to me
You see my pants are something scratchy
Cos they've been in the tumble dryer
Someone swears he doesn't do it
But I know that he's a liar
I'll sit all day at work
With those itchy chafing bloomers
And I can't even relieve it
Well not without starting dodgy rumours
I'll just have to make like a bear
And scratch my bum against a tree
Or shove them in my handbag
When I go to have a wee
Yes I'll have to go commando
If the itch just gets too much
I mean how long can any person stand
An itch they cannot touch
I try to deal with the chair shuffle
But it causes heads to turn
Cos if I do it too much
They might think that I've got worms
What is it makes your sexy pants
Fell like they're made of wire wool
Dragging your ass across the floors not good
For going on the pull
So I'm going to stick with enormous ones
Nice soft ones like my granny
Cos life's too short to tolerate
An itchy scratchy fanny

BAG FOR LIFE

The bag for life torments me
Each time I go for the big shop
It's the one thing you can guarantee
I'll always have forgot
I buy more and more each time I go
I think its some sort of affliction
There's even a whole cupboard
Devoted to them in my kitchen
I've got insulated wine bags
And a range from all the stores
But if I need to give one to someone else
I use the Waitrose ones of course
Because were all secret bag snobs
Come on just admit you are
We all know Lidl and Home Bargains
Are the tackiest by far
There's nowt worse than after forking out
At 50 pence a pop (Morrisons)
The corner of a box pops through
You've bloody ripped it in the shop
Although the placcy bag can be quite handy
For an impromptu picnic
And so long as there's no air holes
It's pretty good for catching sick
So I'll just have to raise my game
To avoid bag related strife
I'll empty the cupboard and fill my car
With a thousand bags for life

EXERCISE

Please don't make me exercise
I really don't want to run
I'm all snuggled up warm in bed
And I've got a note from my mum
I'll have to put the lycra on
Which let me tell you isn't easy
I'll be shagged before I reach the door
Hot and sweaty and slightly wheezy
Once I'm out the door and start

To do my trudging down the street
I'll get burned off by all the young uns
Who leave me staring at my feet
Wondering why I'm such a tortoise
While they bound off like the hare
With their pert buttocks and shiny locks
And condescending stare
They're goddesses in lycra
While I'm trying not to jiggle
When they go by they catch men's eye
Whereas I just make kids giggle
When I hit the hills I grunt and groan
And pull horrible scary faces
Unless someone's coming the other way
Then I stop and check my laces
Sometimes before I run
I forget to go to the loo
Which then gives you the dilemma
Of what should I do
Should I break my personal best
And hurtle home in a rush
Or just take a little detour
And go behind a bush
But what if someone comes along
They'd get such an awful fright
To see me squatting in the bracken
With my pulled down running tights
You see running's fraught with dangers
Embarrassment, flashing and injury
I mean how many runners do you know
Who don't have a dodgy knee?
But I guess I'll keep on running
With my lycra clad big bum
Because as much as I may groan and whinge
You see its actually quite fun
Cos those happy feel-good endorphins
Give your cheeks a lovely flush
Just please proceed with caution
If you see me hiding behind a bush

GETTING OLD

I'm getting old I tell you
I'm knocking on a little
Won't be long till I start knitting
And offering strangers peanut brittle
I'll get a little shopping trolley

Wear a woolly hat all year
And pretend that I can't hear you
Did you say something dear?
They grey hair and the wrinkles
They will win the war
And one day I will realise
I'm much shorter than before
But getting old I reckon
Has some perks along the way
Like wearing enormous knickers
And drinking sherry in the day
I have a theory that these oldies
Are really much more fit and able
After were at work I bet they spend their days
Swapping car keys on the table
A geriatric swingers club
Is going on behind our backs
That's why they never get to the door quick
And daytime telly's cack
The things going on in secret
I think Phil and Holly would blush
All bang at it in their bondage gear
They just keep it all hush hush
And don't start me on the drugs
I bet they've all an impressive stash
They'll be flogging onto kids
To top up that pension cash
And if they don't and actually take it
They must be off their heads all day
They pretend to sleep when you visit
Waiting till they can... partay!
So I'm getting on I tell you
But it sounds like quite a wheeze
I just hope I can keep up with the shagging
On account of my dodgy knees

FARTS

My husband has a gift
Something at which he's unsurpassed
And the gift I am referring to
Is his mighty bottom blast
I'm not quite sure how he does it
So consistently each day
There more be something in his diet
Perhaps he's been eating hay
There's definitely a farmyard smell
It's a nasty niff for sure
I've been out checking neighbour's gardens
For a covering of manure
He has a full on repertoire
From SBDs to trouser rippers
And the smells, well let's just say
I d rather sniff fermented kippers
He lets them go in public
He doesn't care who is around

And makes no attempt to muffle or contain
His farty sounds
It gives him lots of pleasure
Dropping his guts among a crowd
With a smile upon his face
As he revels in his mustard cloud
Quite frankly it repels me
Its awfully sad but true
I wait for the day he comes a cropper
And he finally follows through
I tell him go do it in the toilet
Its really not that hard
But even when he does
The smell travels 20 yards
Maybe he should go on telly
Perhaps his talent will make him famous
I really wish he would go somewhere
Him and his offensive anus
I'm not a prude I know it's definitely
Better out than in
I just with out was 20 miles away
That and the evil sphincter of sin
So if there's any of you out there
Fancies your chances with this lassie
Just perfect your toilet manners
And ensure you're not too gassy

ENERGY PRICES

So the summer is at an end
and the chilly days are here
but I can't afford to put the heating on
the gas and electric are too dear.
In the office I'd be nice and warm
but working at home I'm using my fuel
And I've not had a pay rise for years
looks like I'll soon be eating gruel.
Some bright spark said the other day
just put on an extra layer
but it's hard to type in mittens
but he didn't seem to care.
If someone had said on zoom meetings
we would be wearing a hat and scarf
I'd have thought they were joshing
are you having a laugh?
But it's true I tell you, I've done it
the fact I had to left me raging
what state is our country in
if I have to go to work dressed like Fagin?
I get up and jump about
just to keep my circulation
but it's not very enjoyable
this Arctic situation.
I try not to boil the kettle too much
so I made a flask of tea
and I'm wearing fleecy socks
and light a candle so I can see.
It's really a sad state of affairs
we're going back to the dark ages
so Boris sort out this inflation
and pay us decent wages.

2 TYPES OF PEOPLE

There's 2 types of people in this world I find
Some are nice and some are nutters
Yes the ones that really wind me up
Are the ones that leave crumbs in the butter
Yes there's really some dirty nasty folk
With disgusting kitchen ways
They'll open and bite a lump off the cheese
Then leave it unwrapped for days
Don't be daft you say
No one does that
It'd be solid as a brick
But I'm here to confirm this shit is true
I live with such a dick
These weirdos have other scruffy ways
That make you want to throttle
Like drink milk straight out of the fridge
Leaving floaters in the bottle
One of the worst offences
That makes my little fists shake
Is leaving in the cupboard
An empty box of jaffa cakes
What's wrong with putting stuff in the bin
Is it really that big a job
To get my snacky hopes up like that
Is cruel you selfish knob!
So I've decided the world
Needs to live by my rules
Yes I know that's a bit controlling
Let's punish those that don't comply
Let's get this campaign rolling
Let's fight for a world that's hygienic and clean
With beautiful crumb free butter
And where my hopes are not dashed when I rummage for snacks
Leaving me raging like some chocolate starved nutter

MURDER MOST FOUL

Today I found a creature
When out walking with my child
It was something very rare
I've never seen one in the wild
It was small and grey and furry
But unfortunately dead
Well it must have been cos
Most things don't really
Last long with no head
I found it in the undergrowth
Among discarded bits of litter
Yes a deceased womble I uncovered
Now don't you dare titter
They're real for sure
For after all what else could that thing be
Laid in the muck, poor little f**k
Poor old Tobermory
How he bit the dust
I simply could not quite deduce
As his corpse lay decomposing
Between a bag of chips and orange juice
I did suspect some foul play
In how he ended up, well dead
There were a couple of dodgy teenagers

Kicking round something like a head
Maybe they lured him in with pop cans
And used johnnies as a trap
Then filled him in and left him
Among the rubbish and dog crap
I couldn't leave him there in such a state
I went to bury him instead
So I poked him with a stick
To see if I could reunite him with his head
It went in deep, I gave that
Floppy carcass a good flick
When to my relief I found
It was a toy I'm such a dick
But just because this time I got it wrong
No morbid thrills
Pick up your rubbish
Don't give those kids
Those easy womble kills

PROPER CAMPING

I do proper camping I do
When I go on a trip
It's a memorable experience
None of that soft electric shit
We sit playing cards and drinking
Into the middle of the night
Till we're bursting and have to go for a wee
With just a torch for a light
Dashing through fields in my flip flops
Hoping not to find
A great big dumpalooga
Other campers left behind
And that's not the only scary thing
You can uncover in the night
Until you've heard screaming badgers
You'll never know true fright
There's a lot of nature out there
And not always on the ground
Like the earwigs that showered on my head
When taking the tent down
Or the toads I shared a groundsheet with
Charlie, Keith and Mick
I thought the ground was sort of lumpy

Till I poked it with a stick
Then it moved around
And started to make a funny croaking noise
I didn't know that I'd got company
With those meaty amphibian boys
You can't beat cooking in the open air
Boiling hot dogs in the rain
Taking half and hour to cook the things
As the weather fills the pan again...and again
And camping fashion is outstanding
In my hoody shorts and wellies
I abandon all hair styling
And leave behind my fancy smellies
Yes the camping me is scary
But I find it so much fun
Where else do you get such amusement
From a thistle in your bum
So forget your fancy jollies
A smelly camper I will be
I'll say sorry now
In case you end up
Pitched up next to me

WHY AM I ALWAYS COLD?

Why am I always freezing?
Can someone tell me that?
I've plenty of insulation
An impressive layer of far
I simply have no circulation
In my hands and feet
And before you all get smutty
No I do not need more 'meat'
At working I'm dressed just like an eskimo
While others wear next to nowt
They're sat dealing with hot flushes
While I'm wearing gloves and a coat
I am a little bit corpse like
You wouldn't want for me to feel ya
And you definitely don't want to get sexy
Unless you've a thing for necrophilia!
So come on give me suggestions
On how I can get warm
You know ones that don't involve rude stuff
In any way shape or form
Ever drinking gin...err medicine
Doesn't seem a good solution
Or shovelling down a spicy curry
Creating nuclear lentil fusion
Maybe I am dead after all
And I'm just in your imagination
I died from a failure to stop
This hypothermic situation
Oh no I am still breathing
I'll just wear a jumper and woolly socks
But if you've any ideas please send them on
Before I end up in a box

POUND SHOP

Have you ever been to the pound shop
A treasure trove of pure delight
You nip in for some bin bags
And come out with tonnes of shite
There's products you find in there
I didn't even know were things
Like diamante ceramic llamas
Between the chargers and selfie rings
Its full of office workers
Buying up notepads by the dozen
Unfortunately most of the customers
Must be closely related to their cousin
I can definitely say the pound shop
Has a unique clientele
Most are easily identified
By their jogging pants and funky smell
Don't get me wrong, I'm not a snob
I love a bargain as much as you
I just don't like the shopping experience
To include the smell of poo
But as traumatic as the shop may be
I just can't keep away
Where else sells plastic egg poachers
And teeny tiny coffee trays
There's that funny that sells CD's
Fit only for the bin
I do think they're missing out though
I'm still waiting for pound gin
There's no other shop in summer
Sells a festive Christmas wreath
Alongside sweets and that weird coffee
That strips enamel off your teeth
So I'm back off down the pound shop
I don't want owt it's just for fun
I'm going to see how many customers
Are showing off their builder's bum

BLISTERS

I can't come into work today
There's a blister on my foot
What are you talking about you skiver?
I hear you complain tut tut!
But honestly it's a big one
I've a picture on my phone
My evil shoe ate a chunk of me
I think I can see bone
Every time I put my foot down
I'm overwhelmed with pain
I really cannot walk at all
Just look at the blood stain
I reckon my footwear designer
Is into S & M
I think he likes a bit of pleading
To be set free from them
When I put them on this morning
They felt comfy soft and nice
And yet when I got a mile from home
I think they shrank a size
So I can't come into work today
I can't walk to get the bus
I'll just site at home wearing my heels
Still in pain …but fabulous!

PENCIL

Someone stole my pencil
I left it on the floor
There's no one else been in here
Well at least no one I saw
Perhaps I've got a lurker
Perhaps there's someone here with me
They must've crept right up and nicked it
When I made a cup of tea
I don't know where all my stuff goes
When I take my eye off it
I mean I'm sure I had it with me
But I'm knocking on a bit
Perhaps I had a senior moment
Maybe I never had it here
Oh wait a bit don't panic
I found it tucked behind my ear

PLUMS

I thought I'd pen a rhyme
To bring me into disrepute
It's a little on the smutty side
About men's low hanging fruit
I thought to give them some attention
Might make them a bit more fun
Cos they don't get that much coverage
The lowly trouser plum
Everyone's too obsessed with wieners
And while some are worthy of note
No one seems that keen to share with you
The forgotten little scrote
I think it's because secretly
Most men are a little vain
So they hide their little knackers
Like some pink and saggy brain

They just dangle there all squishy
Just like little buffer pads
But don't underestimate their importance
Where would men be without their nads
They'd have nothing there to fondle
They might start touching us instead
And most marriages couldn't take that
We'd have to send them to the shed
So lets applaud the humble bollock
For keeping our relationships more stable
And us girls will turn a blind eye
When you rearrange them under the table

MEETINGS ABOUT MEETINGS

The workplace is a funny thing

With meetings one after the other
I see more of my work colleagues
Than I do of my own mother
At least not so many are in person
Now I'm not physically there
I just have to dress my top half
Throw on some lippy and brush my hair
To start with we all went bonkers
Over excited to be using zoom
Till we realised everyone could see
The state of our spare room
Then they moved us onto better stuff
We learned by using teams
You could hide the mess behind you
Using different background scenes
You're breaking up, You're still on mute
We frequently will say
But being booted out altogether
Is the highlight of my day
I must say online meetings
Are much better suited to me
You don't wait for folk that turn up late
Then go make a cup of tea
But what do we find to talk about?
The reasons are manyfold
Like having meetings about meeting
Or to not do what we've just been told
We have meetings to prepare for meetings
Or a post meeting review
Or a meeting to remind us
What we've forgotten to do
Cos we're so busy having meetings
We've no time to do our job
So then need another meeting
On how to calm the angry mob
All these meetings are too much for me
I need a lie down in my room
I'll be there in just a minute
Once I've finished on this zoom

POSH

I wish that I were posh
So people would listen to what I say
People tend to think I'm thick
Just because I talk this way
I can't help where I grew up
I'm just a victim of fate
Don't think that I don't know stuff
Just cos I can't talk reyt
I'm sure if I'd gone to public school
I'd use big words and sound full of wisdom
But the main objective at my local comp
Was to keep us out of prison
It's amazing how having a posh accent
Can secure you the top jobs
And us common sorts get left behind
As the mercy of these snobs
In company I'm corrected
On how to say the words I utter
I've a few more I'd like to share with them
The ones straight from the gutter
I didn't play lacrosse or study Latin
And I cannot ride an oss
But I learned not to be condescending
And I do not give a toss
So I may lack some airs and graces
And I cannot speak the lingo
But I'm sure I'll have a better time
Fitting in down gala bingo

YORKSHIRE IS BETTER THAN LANCASHIRE

Yorkshire is better than Lancashire
We all know this to be true
It's the only placed you're guaranteed
To get a proper brew
Plus all our watters better
And our seaside resorts too
We've got lovely sunny Scarborough
But Blackpool's watters full of poo
Descended from hardy Vikings
You'll find no soft jessies here
And just check out Bradfield brewery
You get a proper pint round here
We kick your ass at cricket
And rugby league we invented
Better than that poncy union shite
Sorry if your pride is dented
Weve got the Bronte's Heathcliff Emily Moor
The first British astronaut in space
That and bloody Jean Luc Picard
You can keep your Eccles cakes!
So just keep your side of the Pennines
And you're chuffing hot pot too
Cos we've got Yorkshire pudding
And of course I live here too

AVAILABLE

I'm not saying I'm available
But I'd never say I'm not
I'm keeping my options open
If you're witty kind and hot
They say beauty is only skin deep
It's what really lies beneath

And to be honest I'm not picky
But I'd prefer if you had teeth
I'm not fussy about hair either
Normal grey bald or white
But you really can't be thinner than me
Cos that just wouldn't be right
I know it's such a cliché
But I'm a sucker for kind eyes
And its ok if you're a softie
I love a man that cries
You'd have to tolerate my music
And my singing in the bath
And this may be a deal breaker
But I've got a weird laugh
I can also be quite...assertive
So I'll need to have my way
And I'm afraid that I'll need lots of love
To keep my mood swings at bay
I also come as a package deal
1 teenager and 2 cats
And I sometimes dress peculiarly
I've a thing for funky hats
But if you've got a thing for weirdos
Who like to play in the dressing up box
Drop me a line
Well get on fine
Unless you've got the pox
Oh, I forgot you can't be messy
Angry, stinky or unclean
And no farting in the bed or car
And no wearing leather jeans
So you see I'm quite demanding
For a fat lass with mad hair
I really don't have much to offer
In fact I'm a bit of a nightmare
But if my soul mates out there
Who thinks that sounds like a dream
Them come get me quick I'm waiting
I'm housetrained and very clean

BLIND DATE

I've never been on a blind date

gone to meet unseen men
I don't trust any of my friend's judgement
and how do you know it's them?
Do people really wear a carnation?
and carry a copy of the times?
knowing my luck he'd be a minger
with loads of undiscovered crimes.
You see I'm pretty weird myself
so if anyone tried to make a match
I sort of think he might not be
the perfect catch.
What do you do if he turns up
and he's a state?
do you suddenly feign illness?
or leave him sitting there to wait?
until you found a way
to climb out the window and escape
how far do you need to run
until your getaway is safe?
Do you then call the restaurant
to leave a message so he knows you've gone?
And how long do you wait to do it?
Like until you're safely home?
Cause imagine if he caught you
skipping down the street
revelling in the success
of your hasty retreat?
I suppose then you'd have to marry them
you know, just to put things right
and then after runaway again
this time on the wedding night!
No blind dates are not for me
I'd like to see what I'm gonna get
and not these iffy profile shots
you get on the Internet.
There was that blind date film though
I wouldn't mind if Bruce Willis arrived
but I'm not exactly Kim Basinger
so I think he feel deprived

THE GYM BUNNY

The gym is a beautiful and wondrous place
Where gym bunnies show off their perfection
While young lads hover at the back
With a permanent erection
Carefully positioned to carry out
Those super slow squats and dips
And conveniently braless
So you get a full view of their nips
You're only jealous of them you say
Of course I am! You're right!
If I had ribs and looked like that
My tops would be even more tight
One thing is still a mystery to me
A think I just don't get
They spend hours posing in the gym
Yet never break a sweat
Maybe they've all had that Botox stuff
So I don't think that they can

They wouldn't want it running of their brows
And spoiling that fake tan
But the rest of us ladies
Are there at the back
A sweaty wrinkled army
A dishevelled uncoordinated wobbly bunch
Dressed in old t shirts and Primarni
We don't get the fellas check us out
There's no unwanted advances
United in our mingingness
Free of any admiring glances
Yet we're the real athletes here
Might not look good but we're fit
We get an extra workout
Just dragging round our tits
So our asses might be squishy
With thighs like cottage cheese
And our boobs strapped down to save our eyes
With bad hips and dodgy knees
But don't follow the gym bunnies lads
There's a massive untapped resource
Of real women lurking at the back
If you're easy pleased of course

WAITING TO BE OFFENDED

Sometimes when I'm playing on't internet
My fun is suddenly ended
You know the ones that sit around all day
Waiting to be offended
You make a joke, a glib remark
For fun, no intent
Then suddenly they're at you
They accuse insult and vent
You wonder what just happened
I thought I'd made a joke
But suddenly I'm the devil
According to these folk
I reckon they're not very clever
Miss the humour or subtlety
Then all too soon begin the snide remarks
And say offensive things to me
I'm left confused, bewildered
How can they say this stuff to mwa?
After all I'm nice and lovable
I never take anything too far
I could start annoying them for sport
I like that naughty sort of fun
But I've decided it's too much like hard work
I'll leave their heads stuck up their bum
Let them carry on without me
Let them slag me off and moan
I'm sure they're fully capable of
An argument on their own
I'll just carry on playing on't internet
Well once my egos mended
And they can stay in their little victim mode
Waiting to be offended

DRIVING

I'm going to confess about my driving
Naughty things that I might do
And I guarantee that you'll have done
At least one or two
I don't like to crawl along
I like to make good time
So when some pillocks driving up my arse
It's a little pet peeve of mine
You see, it won't make me go faster
In fact you'll find it quite the reverse
And you'll never overtake me
When I'm feeling quite perverse
You'd be surprised at just how wide
I can make my little car
And I'm happy to play chicken
Yeah I'll take things pretty far
So white van man or boy racer
I'll enjoy getting you riled
As you're impatiently stuck behind me
I'll keep you there for miles
And when I finally let you pass me
I smile and then give you the bird
While you red faced hurl those insults
Like there's nowt I haven't heard!
You see my angry little driver
A little penis head like you
Is just providing entertainment
I just like to play with you
You may think you're a brilliant driver
When you demand to get past
But I think you're safer sat behind me
That way you can kiss my ass

PENIS POACHER

There's lots of penis poachers out there
Liking men's comments on your posts
And when they've finished poaching
They disappear like ghosts
In their bio there's always a pair of jugs
And DM's always open
But I've decided that enoughs enough
Vacate my timeline, I hath spoken!
Why you seem to think my followers
A very discerning crew
Would be interested in conversing
With a skanky trollop just like you
We're here to have a laugh
We don't get up to nothing mucky
I don't want to know if you love them long time
Or if you're offering sucky sucky
It's also bloody lazy to
Build a following like that
It's taken lost of hard work to lure people in
Not flashing them my twat
This poetry I write takes minutes
Of graft and toil I do each day
And you come round here with your hoey ways
Trying to lure my boys away
And worst of all, the thing
That I find really quite disgusting
Is that you think I've got the sort of account
Where you can do your willy rustling
I'm a good girl I am
I ain't no slut
There'll be no saucy shenanigans here
Bugger off with your cams and your only fans
And get your cheap ass out of here

TIRED

You look tired they say
Are you alright?
A polite way of saying you look like shite
I'm sorry I don't look perfect
But I assure you that I'm fine
But honestly what do you expect
From a working mum whose 49?
You know its really not good manners
You're quite the cheeky chuff
Considering you don't know me
To tell me I look rough
Do you go around telling others
They you think they're looking fat
Or that you find them ugly
With a face just like a rat?
You're looking very bald today
Do you know you've got a spot?
Your roots really want doing
Do you say that stuff, why not?
So why is it ok to say
I don't look like you think I should
For heavens sake I'm knackered
I don't care if I look good
So keep your comments to yourself
They don't leave me feeling happy
Cos unless you're a plastic surgeon
I'm stuck here looking crappy

THREAD HOG

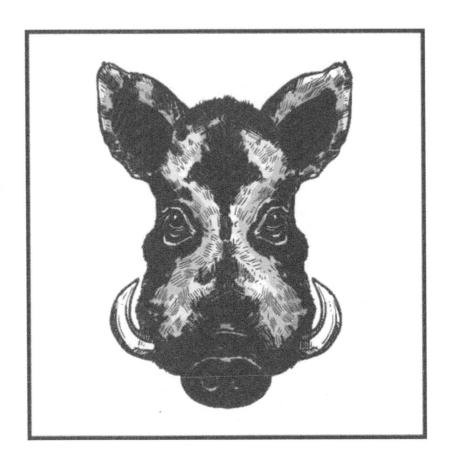

Have you ever had a thread hog
Is it just a twitter thing
You start a conversation
Then someone else jumps in
Its not even related to your post
It snuck in there by surprise
Then you're stuck with having to work your way
Through all of their replies
If you want to start discussions
Make your own little thread
Then you won't be pissing people off

Will all your messages instead
I'm not saying they should zip it
Just keep things where they should be
You put your stuff over there
And I'll keep mine here with me
I don't want to have to mute you
But things are heading that way
I have enough problems keeping track
Of what I get each day
So I've said my bit
Just bugger off your naughty thread hijackers
Don't piss me off or I'll come round there
And kick you in the knackers

POP MUSIC

I had the charts on the other day
and ended up on Radio One
but I wasn't sure when where one song ended
and the other one begun.
I know I am an oldie
and my tastes are odd it's true
which is why I'm normally safely
in the realms of Radio 2.
I don't know much about chart stuff
my chart knowledge is quite tiny
but I do know it's depressing
and also bloody whiny.
What's wrong with all the pop stars
music should be a celebration
if you listen to too much of that
you'll need some form of medication.
It's either 'dance' stuff that I can honestly say
didn't make me shake my booty
in fact I'd much rather have a lie down
as an oldie that's my duty.
And the miserable sod crying about
how his baby left him and he's living in hell
I think she made the right decision
I'd have packed my bags as well!
What happened to pop music
it was fun, catchy and made us smile
now is autotuned bland and dreary
and about as much fun as piles.
I'm going back to Radio 2
and my CDs from times long gone
when music was made with instruments
and we all could sing along.

GIMP

My gimps got out the dungeon
I don't know how he got free
He was chained up tight this morning
And I've still got the key
He must have found the spare one
That I keep in my handbag
I can see how he got his hands free
But he'll never get out that gag
If he's still dressed in his gimp suit
I could be in the shit
People will guess what I've been up to
And what's in my garage pit
It's supposed to be a secret
I keep him locked away
And he does exactly what I tell him
When I bring him out to play
But now my gimps gone rogue
I don't know who to ask
I've forgotten what he looks like
When he's not wearing his mask
I'll just have to get a new one
Someone of a similar ilk

But where do you find someone new
To torture spank and milk?
So if you want to be my plaything
I'm taking applications
You must be clean, local and willing
But strictly no relations
You can't be allergic to latex
Must be up for kinky fun
It'll also be quite handy
If you like things up your bum
You'll find mistress Laura is very nice
She looks after her pets
Except for the blooming missing one
Whose whereabouts I forget
So please forgive my little kinks
I'm just a woman like any other
I just have a thing for naught games
And like my men in rubber

I'VE LOST MY MORAL COMPASS

I've lost my moral compass
I don't know where it's gone
But there's been a definite increase
In the things that I do wrong
I'm getting increasingly naughty
And do things others refuse
Like drinking on a school night
You'll always find me on the booze
At the hockey games I must confess
I have a sneaky look
At the lovely thighs and buttocks
While they're warming up
It may be embarrassing for those with me
But for me, I have no shame
When Big John does his big lunges
Well I think he's the one to blame
I've lost my moral compass
I don't know where it can be
I tried looking down the back of the sofa
But I just found crumbs and a mystery key
My jokes and general sense of humour
Is now toilet level at best
And my ability to resist temptation
Really ought not to be put to the test
I can't guarantee if I get faced
With some horny fit young thing
I won't take full advantage
Open the door and drag him in
So I've lost my moral compass
Perhaps its just a temporary lull
But you won't hear me complaining
Cos this life certainly ain't dull

SCARED OF THE DARK

I'm not scared of the dark
I'm much too told for that
I don't get freaked out easily
Unless attacked by a stealth bat
But the bats are quite cute really
They don't give me a fright
They don't give me the heebie jeebies
In the middle of the night
But getting back in your car at the pictures
After horror movie scares
You can check the back seat all you want
But you're convinced there's someone there
Or walking back home from the pub
When all the street is still
Waiting for the slasher in the bushes
To make you their first kill
In the house it's not much better
When going up the stairs
Once you turn the light off
You know that dicky dark is there
He doesn't want to kill you
But up the staircase you still run
Cos everyone knows when the lights go out
He wants to bite your bum
So apologies if anyone ever tries
To surprise me in the night
I'll be in self defence mode
It'll end up in a fight
So for safety's sake I'd best stay in
I'm much safer at home
And ill make sure when I go to bed
I keep the torch on, on my phone

LADY OF LEISURE

I'm going to be a lady of leisure
because I'm very shagged
the sort of life if you sit down for five
you don't get blooming nagged.
Fetch this for me, go here, get that
don't forget to pick up the other
No I'm having a sit down
and I'm not your bloody mother
I aspire to be the kind of woman
that goes gets her nails done
no worries about breaking them doing the pots
you know purely made for fun.
With lie ins and long lunches
and nothing in between
and no rubbish jobs about the house
cause I'll get someone in to clean.
My hair will be silky and perfectly cut
not with the scissors out of the draw
and when my Botox has worn off
I'll hop in the Jag and get some more.
When I'm tired of lounging around
I'll go on holiday for some fun
and as I'll be there for a month or two
I'll go get my tits done.
Unfortunately I don't have the income
to fund this lavish lifestyle that I seek
I'll have to find me a drug dealer
so I can have nowt to do all week.
So it's back to work and ironing
running kids about and making tea
but do me a favour and occasionally
make a cup up for me.

COUGAR

I need to get me a new hobby
Something to get me out a bit
And I've got the perfect solution
Plus it might also get me fit
I think I'll be a cougar
And snag me some young fella
It'll give the gimp a few nights off
He gets lonely down that cellar
You see the younger ones are so pretty
With their bodies all firm and buff
Just what's needed for us ladies
That cannot get enough
We want men that can keep going
And not stop to have a breather
Or look like they're having a funny turn
Sweating like they've got a fever
A strong young lad with stamina
Whose up for lots of fun
With a pleasing disposition
And a lovely little bum
Yep I think I'll be a cougar
I'll start prowling straight away
I just hope the young s aren't put off
Its not just my eyes that are grey
So I'll check the field out ladies
See if reality fits the dream
And so you don't have to bother
I'll take one for the team

MILFS

Self appointed MILFS and DILFS
Please don't describe yourself as that
Just think what the words really mean
It makes you look a twat
So you really want to do yourself?
Well do one, I think you should
Because your understanding of plain English
Really ain't that good
I know I'm being pedantic
You just want to say you think you're hot
And I'm glad that's true
As one or two
On here might think that you're not
It's great you have that confidence
That despite the fact you sag
You've decided on behalf of us all
You're someone we want to shag
I always thought in terms of sex
I'd at least get a bit of a say
But it seems you've made your mind up
You don't even know if I swing that way
It does seem a tiny bit presumptuous
To think we all want to get in your pants
In fact I'd go as far to say
As it's a little bit arrogant
So please rethink your title
Maybe use your name, hey that's something new
But if you don't and insist on doing it
Then do as you say and go f*** you

CHEEK

Some blokes put rude stuff on my tweets
About collars and cuffs, the blooming cheek!
Its not like you will get a peek
So keep it to yourself
I don't ask you about your willy
Because that's juvenile and silly
And after all I'm a classy filly
Just keep it to yourself
My lady bits are private see
The styling of which known just by me
They'll never be sat upon your knee
I keep them to myself
So keep your comments rude and coarse
Don't push it or I will be forced
To block you and your smut of course
Just keep it to yourself
So please don't think I am a biatch
For being offended if you ask if they match
But you will never see my snatch
So keep it to yourself

MANNERS

You know manners they don't cost a thing
So please use them at all times
Because if you don't you're just being silly
Bugger, there's no clean words that rhyme
Is it so bad to hold a door open
So it doesn't hit me in the face
Or say after you, if there's a queue
Life's really not a race
I think things would be much nicer
If we all just calmed down
And smiled and said hello
Rather than walk round with a frown
Let's sit and talk to the old folk
They might not see anyone else all day
And don't forget please and thank you
When you're asking us to pay
Life could be so much happier
With just a few small changes
You know the world won't end if we take time
To sit and talk to strangers
You might even feel good
If you give your seat up on the train
Or help someone with their pushchair
Things don't have to be such a strain
Come on let's cheer up others
Any maybe some cheeriness will come our way
Let's be that little something
That brightens someone's day
So I'll set the ball rolling
Thank you all for being my mate
You lift my mood each and every day
And I think you all are great...apart from him!

RETWEET

There's something weird going on
It only happens on twitter
People retweet my photos
Between big jugs and someone's shitter
I haven't worked out why they do it
These porn accounts I mean
Why do they spoil their timeline
With my pics they're way too clean?
It just seems kind of creepy
They're sharing me with all their mates
Amid the sort of content
People use to masturbate
Everyone else is nudey
Then there's me in my jumper
Amid slutty minx 2000
And tweets of how they'd like to pump her
I am by no means prudish
Enjoy your x rated fun
But don't stick me in the middle
I'm a slightly aged mum
I don't want to break your rhythm

If you're trying to knock one out
In the middle of all the shagging
I really do stand out
So to avoid me feeling awkward
Like I'm not invited to the party
Please reserve your timeline
For the girls who are more tarty
I feel the odd one out
Sat there in all my clothes
I'm not looking for subscribers
I'm not like those cheeky hoes
If you want to 'use' my picture
Then keep it to yourself
But leave me tucked away
Like your mags from the top shelf
Don't frame my face with boobies
Or surround me with big knobs
And any other sexy parts
You know, their bits and bobs
Just leave me quietly over here
Reciting my little ditties
And I'll keep my woolly jumpers on
With my undercover titties

POSTIE AND THE BEE

The postman just left me a bumble bee
It just lay there on the floor
I didn't know quite what to think
When postie popped it through the door
I don't know if it was a little gift
Made a change from all the letters
Did he slip it in to make me grin
And make me feel all better?
I have a fondness for our fuzzy friends
I think bees are awfully cute
But I'm not sure what he felt about it
As he was thrust through my chute
Did he want a new address?
Was he ready to leave his chums?
All the others are in the garden
Basking in the sun
I couldn't keep him very long
The cats wanted to eat him
So our beautiful relationship
Sadly was quite fleeting
I picked him up inside an egg cup
So I didn't hurt his wings
And carefully explained
My love hadn't waned
But he was meant for greater things
So I returned him to the garden
Where he now lives with the slugs and snails
But he's welcome to come back any time
Just not via the royal mail

MY CATS LOVE ME

I know my kitties love me
And it's a love that's true
Mine made me a special gift
And left it underneath my shoe
Then came to say come find it
We love you so much mum
Just look how much love we've made
Its fresh from out our bum
But its not just fudgy treats they leave
They give moths and spiders too
And they like to mix it up a bit
Not just leaving bits of poo
They know I have a terrible fear
Of the spideys in this place
So they toy with them in front of me
Then fling them in my face
But the best time of day to see their love
Is when their dinners due
Then they tell me most convincingly
We love no one else but you
Sometimes they push the boat out
And bring me pretty things but dead
Like when they got a blackbird
And left it underneath the bed
Sometimes I doubt their motives
And I think it's just cos I have goodies
But then they go and bite folk I don't like
My little gangsta buddies
So I know my cats love me
And they love me more than you
Cos nothing says I love you
Like a steaming fresh doo doo

TALENTLESS

I wish that I could sing and dance
I wish I had some skills
I wish that I have confidence
You know, without booze or pills
Unfortunately I'm too clumsy
I've definitely got two left feet
And rest assured without subjecting you
My singing ain't that sweet
I'm sure somewhere deep inside me
I've a talent I haven't found
It just seems to be so very deep
I think its underground
I long to be creative
Or artistic I some way
But I'm only good at rubbish stuff
Like tidying stuff away

You see people only the telly
'celebrities' they say
They made careers doing nothing
You just have to look a certain way
Maybe my time will come
There'll be a trend
For women of a certain age
Slightly chunky with no talent
But lots of pent up rage
I'd sell my story to the papers
I'd be in every trashy mag you'd see
With a toy boy or three
And tales of debauchery
And a fitness DVD
Maybe that's where I went wrong
I thought you needed some sort of flair
But you just need to be orange
With fake tits and massive hair
But its too late for me
I missed the boat
I'll never be a star
No fancy holidays or bling for me
No diamonds or flash car
I'll never be on telly
Too many things I lack
Unless of course I get my moment
If they bring Crimewatch back
I guess I know my place in life
A hopeless mess I'll be
But if I get a lucky break
Please buy my weight loss DVD

KIDS TODAY

Kids today have got it good
They don't know what bleak is
They didn't have the trauma of
Growing up in the seventies
My first pair of jeans were massive flares
With red buttons on the top

The wind resistance slowed me down
When I was running to the shop
They sent me with pop bottles
For 5 pence back each one
Then I'd disappear for hours
But no one wondered where I'd gone
With a note in my hand from my grandad
20 fags to me they sold
It didn't seem to matter to them
I was only 8 years old
We'd go on all day adventures
Go off with strangers on a hike
Or get a hernia from trying to
Pull a wheelie on our bike
Playing hockey in the rain
In goal with no gloves or pads
Being perved at by paedos at the school gates
And horny teenage lads
Yes school days were quite different then
You learned to take a punch
And that was just the teachers
Who'd been in the pub for lunch
There were ones that hated all the kids
There was an increasing sense of doom
Until he finally exploded
And launched a chair across the room
How we managed to learn anything
With a permanent sense of fear
Is a credit to us all
Just the fact that were still here
So kids you've got it easy
Think yourself lucky you don't get hit
Shut up thinking you're hard done by
You moaning little gits

BORING

Some fella called me boring
He said by poems were rubbish too
I thought it rather rude
And wasn't sure quite what to do
He didn't even know me
He can't know how dull I am
Now my ego has been battered
By the very charming man
I'd show you who it was
Who made the remarks so rude and snide
But I can't do that lovely people
As behind his keyboard he doth hide
I'm sure he's a lovely person
I bet people adore him so
As an expert in all things literary
He's not your average joe
I didn't realise my face and poetry
Were really all that bad
I'll have to do something good to pep them up
So I don't make him mad
I could just sit here and talk about sex like some
But wearing a balaclava
Maybe he'll find that much more interesting
Or I'll just forget the whole palaver
I'll retire and await his offerings
I'll let him take my place
Then I can tell him just how shit they are
If he ever shows his face
But I'd never do that, I'm too nice me
I don't do that trolling shit
I'll just block him and move on
See Ya! You boring little twit

SEX AND DRUGS AND SAUSAGE ROLLS

I got wed when just a young un
a life of domesticity
which means my life is lacking
in some debauchery.
I mean I've had some good times
life's not been one long drudge
but it's less sex drugs and rock and roll
more sat at home making fudge.
I think the sex bits too much pressure
I couldn't let anyone see my bits
you need a certain level of confidence
to hoe around and flash your tits.
The drugs while that's a different case
I've a different tale to tell then
I've always got an impressive stash
of Ralgex and ibuprofen.
I know not quite what you were thinking
Weed, cocaine or PCP
but it really comes in handy
to deal with runners' knee.
I think my lifestyles trending though
Sat at home, eating and getting fat
it's more sex drugs and sausage rolls
because bake off's where it's at.
I'm sure the sexy stuff is not all it's made out to be
and you need to be quite fit
and that's a certain level of maintenance
to which I can't commit.
So I'll keep knocking out the pastry
and working on my buns
and you make sure you keep your hands off
my sticky Sally Lunns

IF I WERE A CAT

If I were a cat I'd like to be

All big round and fat
And sit on my humans lap all day
Observing this and that
But more likely scenario is for me
I'd be scraggy small and thin
And live in an alley that smells of pee
And eat out of the bin
Covered in fleas
There'd be no soft knees
Or cushions and warm hugs
I'd survive on my wits
And eat garbage bits
Drinking puddles and eating bugs
Gazing through the windows
At those lucky pampered moggies
While the rain beats down
And I wear a frown
With my fur all wet and soggy
A sad neglected puss id be
No one would want to take me home
Cos no one wants a manky cat
Full of fleas and skin and bone
My only hope would be someone like me
Looking for a rescue kitty
Who thinks three legs and just one eye
Is really rather pretty
They'd feed me up
And treat me like the princess that I am
And give me sneaky treats all day
Like double cream and Yorkshire ham
And I'll sit staring out the window
And warm my toes up in the sun
Sleeping on their beds all night
And showing them my tum
So if I were a cat
Either thin or fat
I suppose it could be fun
But I think I'll have the best time
If I stay a fat cat mum

ANNOYING HEAD

While scrolling through my twitter feed
A certain lady did appear
She had a most annoying head
And I didn't want it here
I've seen her knocking about before
In a sexy come get me pose
But somehow she doesn't quite pull it off
But its not her body or her clothes
Its because her orb is slappable
Highly filtered and shaped like an egg
With teeny tiny eyebrows
Permanently shocked atop her head
She's not what I'd call ugly
But her features aren't appealing
But the fellas seem to like her
Cos her outfits are revealing
So to stop myself from commenting
And getting myself in trouble
I blocked her and her annoying head
So I don't upset her or burst her bubble
Cos she hasn't really done anything
Apart from offend my eyes
But the temptation to tell her to piss off
Is best removed
I think it's wise
But if I ever see her down the shops
Looking startled and much less smooth
She'd better dodge the back of my hand
Let's see how fast the egg can move
But don't think I'm being nasty
Getting all hard and lairy
I'm just repelled by egg people
I'm ok with meat and dairy

RETURN OF THE GIMP

My gimp came back
I found him curled up
All foetal at my door
He said he's been very very naughty
And could I punish him some more
Turns out that he was lured away
By a willy rustler, there's loads about
But she was too lazy to look after him
So he escaped when she went out
She took away his gimp suit
Made him dress up like a baby
Which isn't what he's into
So he went off that naughty lady
He felt all cold and silly
Sitting all day in his pampers
And longed for the days
When we would play
With gags and nipple clampers
I haven't decided if I'll forgive him yet
His behaviour was a disgrace
I'm going to mull it over
While I'm sitting on his face
I might kick him out
And find myself a new plaything or two
I haven't made a shortlist yet
But I've got my eye on a few
So if you want to be mine
And you can toe the line
And do all I ask of you
Drop me a line
I'll get the twine
And do bad things to you
I reckon you can never have enough gimps
To meet my naughty needs
So come on you lads, or lasses
And I'll treat you to some anal beads

THICK AS PUDDING

I'm not being judgemental
You know I'm not a snob
But there's a lot of people out there
That frankly, are a knob
What went wrong with their schooling
Did they just not go?
How's it possible to function
When your IQ is that low?
I think they went to sex ed though
As they all have 15 kids
I suppose when I was doing homework
They were watching naughty vids

They had focused their attentions
On things less academic
And as a result my village is flooded
With a stupidity epidemic
It makes it hard to socialise
I don't feel that I fit in
It's hard to make conversation
When the lights are on but no ones in
My grandad had a saying for them
And I think it is a good un
You can't educate pork he said
That lots as thick as pudding
But what to do when the dumplings
Are in the majority
Just stay home where its safe I think
And then they can't judge me
Cos judge they do
I see their looks
Like they want to kick my ass
But I don't know why they do it as
I'm really a nice lass
Its not my fault that I can read
And use words they haven't heard
Or had the audacity to get a job
I'm just that stuck up bird
So I suppose the only choice I have
Is to move to somewhere new
Where everyone is cleverer
Then I can be thick as pudding too

DRINK

Why do I get sozzled?
I've asked this over the years
Why do I never stop at tipsy?
And let my morals disappear
If you met me on a normal day
You'd think me warm friendly and trusting
But then I turn into some reprobate
Whose language is disgusting
Of course I don't do this any more
My manners are now more refined
But basically that just because
My booze tolerance has declined
I get pissed on a few glasses
Then I want to go to bed
So I pace myself more steady
So I'm less likely to end up dead
Cos when I'm drunk I get good ideas
And I start collecting strangers
Then I make us have adventures
Which can bring all sorts of dangers
Like nicking random items
Or going to their homes
Or falling asleep in flower beds
Taking dodgy pictures on our phones
So its best that I don't do that stuff
Maybe I should always drive
That should greatly increase my chances
Of getting home alive
I'll start to add in mixers
Just to water it down a bit
It has the added advantage
Of making me act less like a tit
Yes drinking it's not clever kids
To end up like me, you do not want
Waking up in a skip with crazy Bob
And your clothes on back to front

NO PROFILE PIC

There's a very common occurrence on here
It seems to happen to use ladies
We appear to attract attention
From persons best described as crazies
They ask you out
They want to hook up
Yet they never show their face
Yes I'll mee you random stranger

In an unfamiliar place
You seem to have missed the important fact
That although you might like me
I tend not to be attracted to
Mystery people I can't see
I know looks, they're not essential
But let's not pretend they're not a thing
I might not be inclined to shag someone
I find ugly as sin
It seems never to have crossed your mind
I might not fancy you
And I really don't want to partake
In your list of things that we should do
So I do not want your number
And I really don't want to chat
And I'm sure that model on your profile
Isn't you or I'll eat my hat
So give your head a wobble mate
Here's a reality check for you
Just because you think you're fantastic
Doesn't mean women fancy you
And the fact your face is hidden
Just lets us know that you're no good
You're either married or you're scary
So I'll decline your offer bud
But let's not forget the extra special ones
That fall in love from far away
They desperately want to come visit you
But they can't afford to pay
Well I'm sorry to break it to you mate
But I'm really not naive
So if you think that you can scam me
Well tough luck you'd better leave
So I'm not hard up
I've got standards
And I'll never be a sucker
So go try your luck elsewhere lover boy
You cheeky little f**cker!

SMOKERS

Smoking is revolting
Sorry if it offends
And I also feel the same
About those bloody vape pens
It's the smell that really gets me
I don't subject you to my aroma
So don't surround me in a puff of smoke
Unless you wanna end up in a coma
If you really have to do it
Then don't do it near me
Go outside and do it over there
I'd rather be fresh and cancer free
The fag snell just won't go away
Who wants to smell like an ashtray
Or the sickly rancid vape juice
I have to breathe in every day
If you were a tee totaller
I wouldn't make you have a drink
So what gives you the right to poison me
With your toxic dirty stink
So I've finished with my ranting
You go suck on your death stick
Cos you smell and all your clothes do too
And it frankly makes me sick

BLOW UP DOLL

Why does everyone look like a blow up doll?
Tiny waist and massive hips
And a perfectly blank expressions
With those perfect blow job lips
I don't want to be smooth and shiny
I think its over-rated
I'd rather be me
Old and wrinkly
Like I'm just a little bit deflated
I know I pull some funny faces
And my foreheads full of lines
But I look like me
Which is ok you see
Cos being older is just fine
I'm used to people asking if I'm tired
Which is code for you look rough
But I'd rather that than fill my face
With that bloody Botox stuff
I don't want to be expressionless
How would people know when I was sad?
And folk need some way of knowing
If they've made me really mad
They can retreat to a safe distance
Before they get too near
Just by reading the looks I'm giving out
Then come back when the coast is clear
And don't start me on those implants
In your boobs and in your bum
Cost they just look plain ridiculous
And squeezing them can't be much fun
They must have very little sensation
At least mine are the real deal
Heading south, but they're nice and squishy
Look, come and have a feel
So I'll keep my bits just as they are
No sex doll look for me
And better still I don't wear out
After the 12 month guarantee

MY BAG

I'll let you have an insight
Into the things that can be found
In the bottom of the handbags
Us ladies drag around
It's been a well kept secret
We never let you have a peek
And you must be really careful
If you poke around too deep
There's a pack of little hankies
In every mums bag guaranteed
To deal with snotty noses
And in case of outdoor wee
A bit of lipstick in a shade
That never suited me
That explains why it's been hanging around
Since 1993

A couple of plasters
A worn out pen
And some of them I'm brave dentist stickers
And just in case the day gets better
A spare pair of fresh knickers
For some reason a lonesome paperclip
Entangled in some tights
A hair brush with bobbles round the handle
And that cream for cuts and bites
So you see it's no wonder
Our bags are immense
We keep it on hand
So were prepared for all events
A serious word of caution though
I know it sounds exciting
But don't eat anything you find in there
No matter how inviting
There's mints right at the bottom
From the beginning of time
And stray crisps which if I'm honest
I don't even think are mine
So with this new found knowledge
I've probably told you quite enough
To realise we carry loads about
So you can carry your own stuff

WORKING FROM HOME

I will get dressed fully every day
Not just my top half
I'll make time in my meetings, to chat and have a larf
I'll tell myself it's ok to take a break, or miss a call
And I'll keep my desk clean and tidy and not stick post its on my
wall
When I have lunch I will go to the kitchen and stop eating at my
desk
And I'll put gaps between my meetings, to stop us all from getting
stressed
I'll remember people are only human, and they might need breaks
too
And not keep calling them repeatedly
They might have just nipped to the loo
So these are my rules for working from home
You can share if you agree
But don't call me back, I wont answer
Because I've just nipped for a wee

FOOD THAT ISN'T FOOD

Do you ever wonder about some food?
You know food that shouldn't be
Some things were never meant to be eaten
Like eels and beef jerky
I mean jerky you can't even swallow it
It gets caught up round your clacker
And I don't believe its proper beef
I reckon its some poor bullocks knacker
Then there's black pudding which is dried up blood
A scab upon your plate
Touching all the breakfast food

Trying to contaminate
Ok I don't like my food touching
I like things neatly side by side
Not so the juices can infiltrate
What touches what I will decide
But I digress, I was talking about
Those foods that shouldn't be
Like liver, for heaven's sake it's got tubes!
And why would anyone eat kidney?
The wars over mate
And rationing too
Let's take offal out the mix
There's lots of lovely food out there
We don't need stuff that makes us sick
But don't get me wrong
Its not just weird meaty bits that should be banned
The vegan stuff is just as bad
Not everything's nice that's grown on land
I don't deny its colourful
Some look amazing to the eye
Its just other senses like smell and taste
That tell me to deny
How anyone can tell me those funny green things
I don't know if they're beans or peas
Are ok for human consumption
I'd rather eat a plate of bees
So if you see me looking queasy
Its cos I'm faced with something scary
Keep your meat and vegan stuff to yourself
I'm staying safe with dairy

BUGS

Sometimes when I feel gloomy

And I'm fed up being me
I think its probably not as bad as being a bug
You know like a flea
I mean a flea's life's pretty rubbish
People attack them with combs and sprays
When they're really only having dinner
It's just their bitey little ways
Or when you're feeling lonely
And you really need a hug
I don't see anyone queuing up
To cuddle or hug a slug
I know bees are small and cute
You can't deny they're pretty things
But still everyone just runs away
Cos we're terrified of their stings
They sit there on the pavement
All tired out from pollen stealing
And we all just stare and leave them there
Never caring how they're feeling
Perhaps they just want to be our friends
And maybe even spiders too
But we just squash them in some bog roll
And flush them down the loo
Or the lonely little blue bottle
For whom my feelings of love have stirred
I think I'd let him stay with me
If he'd stop feasting on that turd
And Mr fuzzy caterpillar
Slowly travelling down my path
He only wants to move along
And make it to the grass
But instead kids come pick him up
Poke him, stroke him, oh how they laugh
But then suddenly it all goes sour
When he leaves them with a rash
So I feel sorry for our bugly friends
The lonely caterpillar bug and flea
Cos life's given them a pretty bum deal
When it's better being me

GOING ON HOLIDAY

We are all dying to go on holiday
A week or two in the sun
All desperate to burn our white bits
Including that bit under your bum
Its hard to tan all over
When some areas cast more shade
And you know if you get strap marks
They'll take all year to fade
So everyone sees your spreadage
Especially us with ample tits
We've achieved that perfect all over tan
Except for our arm pits
We all start drinking like were Oliver Reed
On those all-inclusive deals
With pina coladas with breakfast
And the other hourly meals
Its oh so easy to over indulge
There's only one thing to say
When anyone says haven't you had enough?
No I'm on holiday!
I want to be tipsy all the time I'm there
I want to sleep all day
I want my skin to glow in the dark
I'm on holiday!
I know there's great activities
I really should do a class
But its so hot and I'm so comfy here
Unless it can be done lying down I'll pass
Just get me to a cabana
Butler service for my needs
If we're lucky well get the dodgy one
That can score us the good weed
Yes we'll party like were loaded
Drink our money's worth of champagne
Then after a few months dieting
We'll do it all again

WRONG DEMOGRAPHIC

While watching telly the other day
I noticed something strange
There's a certain group that doesn't exist in ads
Its ladies in my age range
It would seem when approaching fifty
Were no longer seen as mums
Oh no forgive me there was an ad on there
It was special pants for leaky bums
I didn't realise I was about to lose control
Better get something absorbent between my thighs
And get the special life insurance in place
For my imminent demise
But apart from that were not to be seen
Our demographics not reflected
Which is really rather foolish
To leave us feeling all rejected

Believe it or not us older gals
Contribute to society
But I'm not gonna spend my cash with you
If you keep ignoring me
I shall reject your cheapo fashion
And you can shove your fast food
If I'm just a pissy wrinkled old woman to you
You can see you've put me in a mood
Just because were not smooth and beautiful
Or are the perfect size
You've deleted us from society
As we must offend your eyes
So I get the hint
I'll start shopping from
Those leaflets in woman's own
Ill spend my days wearing beige
With elastic waistbands like some old crone
But don't think you can win me back later
When you want to sell denture fixer
Or that face cream Helen Mirren flogs
That requires a cement mixer
You had your chance and blew it mate
You wrote me off way too fast
I'm off to work to change the world
And hopefully kick your ass

DM SLIDERS

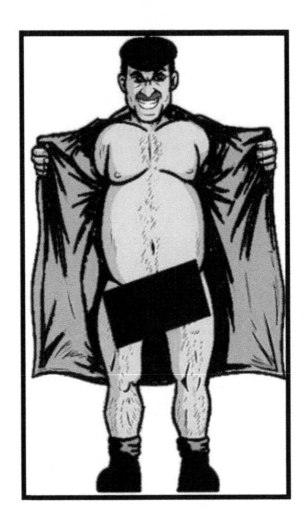

I did a little experiment
I flashed a bit of skin
Then sat and watched my DMs explode
As the sleazy ones slid in
It was a bit naughty on my part
Sort of a honey trap
But I just wanted to block the pervs
Rather than listen to their crap

I'm not your babe
I'm not your hun
That might work on silly girls
But I'm a lady and a grown up dear
A woman of the world
I've heard it all before you see
Its not my first time round the block
And I don't want what you're offering
Especially not your tiny cock
It appears the art of conversation
Is well and truly deceased
In fact its so far gone in your case
Someone ought to call a priest
Your crude attempts at flattery
Turn quickly towards shagging
And I bet you're rubbish at that too
2 minutes and you're flagging
So if you've something nice to say
And you're respectful come on in
But if you're crude and sleazy mate
You're going in the bin
There's lots of sites for you out there
With girls up for titillating
I think you're better off on Tinder
You'll find them accommodating
And I'm not stuck up or snobby
But you'll never get a date
Cos I don't know if anyone's told you
You're trying to punch above your weight
You're really not a looker
And your conversation skills are weak
But guess what you're good at something
You're my minger of the week
So I'll leave it there my point is made
Sorry to be blunt my old mucker
And just to be clear
I'm not your dear
And I certainly ain't no hooker

SUMMER

Its summertime the sun is out
Where are my shorts and sandals?
Its time to tan our white bits
And flaunt our love handles
There'll be fellas with their beer guts
And lasses with muffin tops
Either shirtless with a t shirt tan
Or like a sausage in flip flops
What happens when the sun appears?
We lose our sense of style
We throw clothes and caution to the wind
Wearing little more than a smile
Parading round the local shops
Showing off our tanned physique
Suddenly everyone's half naked

And showing off their manky feet
People's feet they don't half freak me out
I know they need to cool them when its hotter
But I do feel sort of queasy
Seeing a sandal clad pigs trotter
And your boobies get all sticky
And your waists all sweaty too
When you finish your work for the day
The bras off! Just your pants will do!
Although please remember others
When in these states of undress
We don't want to cause the neighbours
Unnecessary distress
Especially that bloke from 42
He's got a telescope behind the drapes
I don't know what he does in there
But I think he's got the shakes
And let's not forget the beer supplies
We have to buy a pack each day
And those G&Ts in the garden are a must
To keep dehydration at bay
You can't find a sausage for love nor money
Or those pesky barbeque bricks
They get snapped up in the morning
And were just left with that vegan shit
But it doesn't matter anyway
As my cooking skills are poor
It's either burnt or raw, or both sometimes
And it's probably been on the floor
So, summers pretty grim it seems
As are our summer ways
But I suppose we can't get too upset
It'll be gone in a few days

DIET

I've gone on a diet
I need to shed some lard
So I'm limiting what I'm eating
Because exercise is hard
There is a minor problem though
As I really like my treats
So ill probably get pretty mardy
Without chocolate and sweets
Why is it all the healthy stuff
Tastes of cardboard and despair
I've cleared out all the sugar and carbs
So soup and salads all that's there
I do ok I start the day
Full of muesli fruit and such
But usually by 3 o'clock
Its all got a bit much
Eating the chocolate chips out of cereal
And the peanut butter out the jar
And searching though my handbags
For an abandoned chocolate bar
I know I should have a banana
But it doesn't do the trick
Unless it's dipped in Nutella
I guess I'll just have to stay thick
I hear curvy is still popular with some
So I think I might not risk it
As someone could get injured
In my frantic search for biscuits
So in the interest of public safety
I'll not bother trying to get thin
I'll sit here fat but harmless
With a mars bar and some gin

MY NEIGHBOUR

I live next door to a madman
Who is obsessed with DIY
Spends all his time in his garage
But if you see his wife you'll know why
He's up at the crack of dawn
With his drilling banging and sawing
He spends no time with her indoors
Although she does seem pretty boring
In fact you can hear her halfway down the street
With her annoying cackle
So I suppose he's better in the shed
Fiddling with his tackle
At least he's safe there from the nagging ways
Of his trouble and strife
I'm just a bit concerned he might be in there
Sharpening his knife
One day he'll have had enough
Something in his mind will blow
And years from now we'll find her brookie style
Under the patio
But I'm sure he'll have done a lovely job
When the missing persons squad come checking
They'll have to admire his handiwork
While they're ripping up his decking
But I think he's doing woodwork now
A lovely big long box
Although he was mumbling something about
Weighing it down with rocks
But I think she's safe
At least for now
He's not ready to fix her
But I'll be watching closely
When he fires up the cement mixer

ADS

Get them up there girls!
That's the latest Tampax ad
What absolute pillock thought of that?
Are they raving mad?
Its not my favourite pastime
I can think of better things to do
That practice shoving cotton wool
Up my lady flue
But this ad it got me thinking
Will other companies do it too?
Start telling us quite crudely
All the things their products do?
There's one for the boys that's straight to the point
if she gives you a chubber
shove on a rubber
or one for those that need to anoint
slap our lotion on your piles
you can cycle for miles
There's others in mind in a style of this kind
leaky bladder? Really?

Wear these pants and pee freely
Or with parents in mind and their babies behind
If your kids are extra crappy
Try our reinforced nappies
I think this advertising malarkey's
a piece of piss
They stuff they churn out
Is no better than this
And I think you will find
My language is finer
As I don't tell you to shove things
Up your vagina
But if you want to
That's all very fine
But I'm going to stick
With my bottle of wine
Get it down you girls!

NEW YEAR'S RESOLUTION

As the new year approaches
resolutions spring to mind
as we look back on what we've been like
and what should get left behind.
I'm not going to do that diet stuff
I'm way too fond of cake
and don't even think about me giving up gin
that'd take less than a day to break.
I'm already pretty active
so I'll give exercise a miss
and I'm not in a position to give up work
although that would be bliss.
Giving up your family's frowned upon
they tend to follow you about
although there are a couple
I could really do without.
How about giving up cleaning
I could give up ironing too
although I think with resolutions
that's not what you're supposed to do.
I could give up sex
but is that how I want to live?
I suppose I could attach conditions
like it just depends who with.
I could give up writing rhymes
but I'd just get up to no good
although I reckon there's plenty out there
Who think I really should
I've got it! I know what resolutions
I am going to make
I'm going to give up resolutions
pass me a slice of cake

SOMETHING ON THE CEILING

There's something dark on the ceiling
I think I ought to warn you
I've been watching it a while
But now it's coming out the corner
I can't work out what it is
It's definitely some sort of creature
I'm sure it's really very nice
But bug, I've no desire to meet you
It's not moving very fast
I'm sure I can outrun it
But I've got my slipper close to hand
In case I need to stun it
It's going to stop me going to sleep
It's every move I need to track
It was heading for the window
But now it's coming back
I can't tell if it's a spider

Or some other sort of pest
But either way its going to have to leave
Before it makes a nest
Or crawls into my mouth
In the middle of the night
We all know what you wake up choking
That's what happened right?
It might want to bite me
Or lay eggs under my skin
That burst out when they hatch
Oh Christ I need another gin!
We're going to have to deal with it
I've all the lights on in the house
I'd much rather it was something
Cute and furry like a mouse
But no, I have mystery egg laying bug!
My evil bedroom invader
If I can't be rescued soon
I'll have to get a neighbour
But then if I go next door for help
I might lose track of its location
And with assistance here but no bug near
I'll get a reputation
I'm just going to have to stay awake
Until it leaves or dies
The only problem is I'm really tired
But I just can't close my eyes
So I'm sending out an SOS
Please come quick I need my bed
But be careful when you reach the door
It's right above your head!

BORED

I'm bored, I've got nowt to do
There's nothing on the box
I'll end up from now to bedtime
Just staring at the clock
Do a puzzle you say
Or read a book
Or perhaps learn to knit
But I'm on my arse all day at work
I really don't want to sit
I've been stuck inside all day
Doing housework for hours on end
And now its time for something else
Before I go round the bend
But there's not much to do round here
Even the ironings done
I want someone to take me out
For a drink and have some fun
I don't want to talk about politics
I'll only get irate
And we may find that we don't agree
Then you might not be my mate
I'm not much good at making things
I'm not the crafty sort
And apart from my morning runs
I'm not that good at sport
I'm even worse at DIY
I think you should do it instead
So perhaps I should just give up
And just go to bed
At least if I'm bored in bed
I'll be comfy safe and sound
But if you think of something fun to do
Be sure to come around

TWITTER IS IN CODE

I think perhaps I've cracked it
The subject of this ode

Is to share with you my thinking
That Twitter is in code
All the things people say they are
They clearly are not
Like the ones that go to such great lengths
To tell us that they're smoking hot
I'm so horny for you
Come spank me now
I need your sole attention
Roughly translates as desperate, alone
With some sexually transmittable infection
And for those who say how funny they are
Then post stuff that's offensive or crap
You're really about as funny mate
As a dose of the clap
You may be crazy and funny
But not in a humorous kind of way
More ward 10 type of crazy
That should be locked away
You see funny it should make us laugh
And your banters just plain rude
And sexy? Well you just don't get it
You're just sat there in the nude
So I'm pretty sure you're not well hung
As your bio seems to claim
My moneys on a micro penis
And just a little bit well…lame
Cos posting pictures of big willies
It's not normal you know
It's not the way to meet a lady
Unless you're looking for a hoe
So basically the secret to twitter
Is take everything they say
Then flip it on its head
Cos its probably the other way
So with this all in mind
And everything's the opposite of what we claim
Id like to say, I'm tall and thin and funny
And not the slightest bit insane

KNOB CHEESE

I've heard it on good authority
Some will deny and others cackle
That some of you fellas out there
Hardly ever wash your tackle
It's really quite disgusting
Only once or twice a week
I mean you have to clean your pee pee
Otherwise it'll reek
And let's face it, its not a pleasant smell
Your whiffy rancid junk
Women aren't turned on at all
By pants that smell of funk
It only takes a minute
To make him and his supporters clean
And I don't mean just dip it in the sink
Go over round and in-between
Surely in the summer heat
Things get proper yucky
And I reckon they must stick to your leg
Those sweaty little chukkies
So on behalf of all us ladies
I'm asking pretty please
Wash your danglies at least once a day
Cos no one likes knob cheese

49 NOT OUT

I'm 49, I'm not dead yet
Please don't put me in a rage
Because I actually may blow a fuse
If someone says you look good for your age
What on earth is that supposed to mean
A compliment but only just
Like an old car fixer upper
Just a bit battered with a touch of rust
I never cease to be amazed
How young uns write us off so soon
I might be ancient to you matey
But I've only just started to bloom
With age so comes wisdom
Well for some of us at least
So don't read me the last rites quite so soon
I'm a long way off deceased
I've earned my stripes and I know my stuff
The latest model I'm definitely not
But don't kid yourself if you think I can't
Be clever, shrewd or hot
Because when your balls have dropped
You'll see us mature ladies deserve the attention
And teenage girls are just too needy
With insecurities too many to mention
We have style and our own money
And we've heard it all before
So you'll have to try a bit harder love
If you want to score
You see the vintage look is back
And that goes for fellas too
Id rather have a silver fox
That a silly kid like you
So next time before you comment
Think! Its really not that hard
And just ask your mates, cos they don't think
Your mum's ready for the knackers yard

RIDICULOUS TWEETS

I try to behave on here
I don't post comments that offend
But there's people out there posting stuff
That are clearly round the bend
There are those that are so bland
I don't know what response they are after
What did you have for breakfast?
Had me doubled up with laughter
I mean what do you say to that?
Not a lot of truth be told
I don't think they want to hear about sausage time

With a twenty five year old!
But then others go the other way
Felt cute, might suck some dick
Is that really the best you've got my dear?
It makes you seem a little thick
And I don't think you are helping with
Retweet if you wanna see my ass
I'll be honest with you lovey
You're not exactly exuding class
But at least your cries for attention
Although crude and a bit too mingey
Aren't as bad as the others
Which are just plain cringey
This is what 35 looks like
Which is just fishing, I can see the hook
To be honest you look a bit rough mate
Even though you're filtered to fuck!
I might try it the other way round
And knock 20 years off my age
Then when people tell me I'm ugly
I'll fly off the handle in mock rage
I can cry about it then block them
Just before they block me
Then share their details with all and sundry
And soak up sympathy with glee
I would say please don't post like this
But it is a source of fun
And I promise I won't make comments
Ill just ask are you ok hun?

SEASONS

It's Christmas time or it nearly is
time for me to start a list
it's not for presents or owt exciting
just what I'll need to get pissed.
You see all these things that happen through the year
Easter, Christmas or holidays
just mean more time spent with the family
and their annoying ways.
It doesn't seem 2 minutes since we were in the garden
hiding easter eggs for our hunt
I still keep finding the odd one cos
that Easter bunny's a tricky… chap
Then it's Halloween, which I do enjoy a bit
cause I like chasing the kids away
as I'm a bit of a git.
Why should they have all the fun
I don't want to be Dracula's wife
I want to jump out of the shadows
in a balaclava with a knife!
That'll give them a surprise
they deserve a proper fright
makes them less inclined to say penny for the guy
when it's bonfire night.
But Christmas is the best by far
We're okay before the big day
but once the big one's over
we're ready to go our separate ways.
I can see why they spread the holidays out
sort of big one for each season
so we don't see the family all that much
and that's a bloody good reason.

CHEMIST

The chemist is a terrible place
Where every visit is like a confession
And in order to make your embarrassment complete
They use all the skills in their possession
I'm at the counter scanning for pills
I can't see them my stomach churns
I whisper discretely to the girl on the till
Then she shouts, what do we give for worms?
They're not for me I hastily add
As I stand there looking vexed
Trying to pretend I came for something else
Quickly grabbing lube and ribbed Durex
Is there anything else? she asks loudly
As I mutter cough and blush
But now she seems unable to hear, so I yell
Have you got anything for thrush?
It's strange but some products get you judged
While others get you pity
And they seem to serve you quicker
If you need things to make you less shitty
Yes diarrhoea pills get you sympathy
And the other one everyone avoids
You'll get 'I've been there' looks and glances
When you buy cream for haemorrhoids
But the worse thing of all, I've ever had
Is going in there in a hat
To cover up home hair dye jobs
That left me looking like a twat
Yes I know my hair is orange
It was supposed to be blonde I know
It was a stupid idea so point me to the brown
And away I'll go
So if you work in a chemist
Please don't make us feel ashamed
Cos if we've worms, piles thrush and diarrhoea
Were already in enough pain

KIDNEY STONE

Oh tiny little kidney stone
Residing in my gut
I know you're only little
But you're like passing a coconut
I know you've grown attached
We've been together for a while
But I now can only grimace
I've forgotten how to smile
Its time to move on little friend
I wish you happiness and luck
But you're hanging around in a painful place
I think you may be stuck
You need to find a new home
We need to find some sort of lube
That will move you on to pastures new
Instead of my wee wee tube
I drink gallons of water and herbal tea
To try alleviate the pain
But now I've forgotten how to pee
And yet here you remain
I'm sloshing about in agony
Something's got to give
And I'm afraid its you so bugger off
You've a whole new life to live
But in the meantime I'll just sit here
With the hot water bottle on my tummy
Drinking water like there's no tomorrow
And feeling pretty crummy

NIGELLA

I think I'm going to learn to cook
Get kitchen skills just like Nigella
That way I can get an upgrade
For a better class of fella
Maybe that's where it all went wrong
Why I haven't got a cultured man
Is that my idea of fancy food
Is chips egg and spam
I didn't do domestic science
I never learned sexy ways in the kitchen
I did mod tech with all the lads
And built a home security system
No one told me doing that stuff
Wouldn't blow the lads away
Well except for the one that got 240 volts
When he got in the way
I've never been a girly girl
I don't possess the attributes
That appeals to posh rich blokes
With fancy cars and swanky suits
It's a certain kind of woman
Gets all the good breaks in life
And I'm afraid I'll never be anything like
One of those trophy wives
You know I think cooking like Nigella
Just won't cut the mustard
And I don't really want that lifestyle
I'm sure she's always getting busted
So Nigella you can have the millionaires
All the cash and fancy parties
And you can take your mystery ingredients
And shove them in your mic-ro-wah-veh!

SHOP LOCAL

Shop local they say it creates jobs
Keeps the locals out the gutter
But everyone forgot to mention
Local shops are full of nutters
Who are you looking at you effing nonce?
Some psycho yelled across the store
At some poor lad only came in for custard creams
And he chased him out the door
I suspect the chap in question
May have had some coke, and not the fizzy sort
Unless he's usually paranoid and aggressive
And hunts teenagers for sport
But him strutting round like he's ten men
Wasn't the only treat today
There was the chap in the queue in front of me
With him bum cheeks on display
I don't know if it was intentional
A sexy look he was going for
But his wangers weren't the cleanest
And his trousers nearly on the floor
It was awful I couldn't look away
My eyes fixated on the spot
Taking in the naked horror
Of his saggy sweaty bot
I must say my experience was enhanced
By the 'lady' on the till
Who coughed all over my shopping
Then told me she was ill
And the kids outside sat on my car
Gave me such a sense of delight
As I gently encouraged them to move
Whilst avoiding a gang fight
So I don't think I'll shop local
I'll go where my life is in less danger
And I don't get flashed or infected
Or threatened by some drug fuelled stranger

MY LITTLE BOOK OF MEDICINE

I know everyone's an expert
On how to cure all our ills
But my nursing skills are all you need
There's no need for drugs and pills
I have 3 cures that can be used
In any situation
And not a single one of them
Requires medication
The first one you will all recall
From school, they had it right
Just put a paper towel on it
Works for grazes cuts and bites
If it's a knock on the head you'd better wet it
So you don't get an egg
And you might need a couple of extra ones
If you accidentally chop off a leg
My second cure I tend to use
For lumps bumps and dislocations
Whatever's sticking out, just push it back in
There's no need for operations
If it won't go back
You'll have to deal with it
There's no need for a grumpy face
Just accept that sometimes kneecaps
What to live in a new place
The final cure is my favourite
Don't cry and be an ass
Just stop bloody whining
And wait for it to pass
Stop rolling round like some jessie
Clutching your stomach or your head
We all know it's the quite ones that are hurt the worst
Especially if they are dead
You might think I sound uncaring

But try them out you'll see
Then you can be a proper nurse
And cure people just like me
But the thing you must remember
If your patients in a mess
Don't forget you can still cheer them up
In your special nursey dress

MY CAT IS BROKEN

I think my cat is broken
He's behaving rather odd
He's gone to sleep inside my pillow slip
The cheeky little sod
He said he wasn't moving
So I snuggled up really near
And he started nuzzling gently
Then tried to lick inside my ear
I know some folk like that kind of thing
But I found it pretty disturbing
Especially when he got all frenzied
And tried to pull out my earring
But its not just his behaviour
That makes me think he's bust
He's some horrid toilet habits
My stinky little puss
He may have exploded several times
It's not funny don't you dare laugh
And when he'd filled up his litter tray
He left some in the bath

Which I suppose was quite considerate
His kindness did improve my mood
Well that was until I went downstairs
And found his regurgitated food
But I really couldn't tell him off
With his eyes so big and round
He seems to think I should be pleased
With all the gifts he left around
But although my cat is broken
He knows that I still care
Cos I'm a little bit broken too
So we are the perfect pair

RAMPANT PERVERSION

I know we all use social media
As a little pastime or diversion
But who'd have ever thought there'd be
So much bloody rampant perversion
Which got me onto thinking
Where did people go for kicks?
Before the online constant stream of sex
How did the pervs get their fix?
I mean there were always the ones at the school gates
Armed with sweeties trying to get lucky
The ones you were told to run away from
If they said, would you like to see some puppies?
I have had the misfortune
To have been flashed more than once
But apart from that the only perv I know
What that teacher we found out was a nonce!
So what were the rest up to
Buying top shelf magazines
And renting from specialist video shops
Stuff strictly for over 18s
But that lot are easy pleased
What about the ones that like tights or feet?
Were they doing stuff in shoe shops
Or out there in the street?
And how did people find out about S&M?
How did they learn how it was done?
And where did they buy their toys
And things for up their bum?
There's no denying that the internet
Is a constant source of inspiration
And it keeps the perverts safe at home
Whatever their inclination

POLITICIANS

I've come to the conclusion
All the affairs and copulation
Are something you only access
With a private education
I mean at work, I work
I can honestly say
I've never had an offer
To …play away
Unlike these politicians
Who are subject to scurrilous rumours
Of goings on behind closed doors
And getting in their aide's bloomers
I've never had a sniff off it
Office parties hold no hope for me
No dodgy going on in the copy room
Or caught on CCTV
If I'm honest I'm quite insulted
I didn't think I was that bad
Even these inbred public schoolboys
Get more chance of a shag
I don't know where they get the energy
To undertake all this seduction
You think they'd be run off their feet
With their other acts of corruption
Perhaps my standards are too high
I just can't go for some MP or leader
With their acts of moral turpitude
And they're all such ugly bleeders
So please stop with all these stories
Of MPs and their misplaced affections
I really can't cope with the thought
That they ever had an erection

LITTLE FLY

Little fly upon my leg
Just in case you haven't heard
You really ought to go away
Because I'm not a turd
Are you telling me I'm stinky?
Do I taste nice? Is that true?
Because you seem obsessed with sitting on me
Do I really smell of poo?
You've been buzzing round the house all day
Always seem to be where I'm at
But if you don't buzz off pretty soon
I'll introduce you to my cat
And why is it when you fly around
You fly about in a square
So I get obsessed with following you
Here there and there and there
You're sending my eyes bonkers

And although you're only tiny
I can hear you over the telly
Your little voice all small and whiny
I opened up the window
To help you escape from within
But you got all angry and bounced off the glass
Went outside then flew back in
I really don't want to splat you
I like things nice and clean
But if you don't depart
You're going to get
Well acquainted with this magazine
So little fly, be a good guy
Leave me alone for a bit
Just go to him over there on the sofa
If you want a real big shit

THE ZOO

I love to go to the zoo
There's loads of ways to be silly
Like going in the monkey house
Trying not to laugh at their willies
You see the mums and dads in there
Stifling the giggles
While the kids all look on innocently
Mum what that long thing in the middle?
And while we're on the subject
Have you ever seen
What lucky Mr Zebras
Got going on in between?
No wonder Mrs Zebra's
On the other side of the field
She's keeping safely out the way
Until her lady bits have healed
But that's not the only source of amusement
You can have hours of fun
Watching the tiger enclosure
As parents offer up their son
Look he wants to eat you!
They tease and laugh with delight
While their little kid is traumatised
And paralysed with fright

Just imagine the size of it to that poor kid
That growling, prowling beast
While the parents look on mocking you
Saying you'll be its next feast
I personally like the reptile house
You can't beat a nice long snake
Or looking at the turtle's heads
Sorry these lines were just too easy to take
In fact there's so much scope for
Innuendo with beavers and cocks I've found
There's plenty of ways to have a giraffe
And simply horse around
I'm sorry I've have taken it all too far
My animal jokes were lame
But be free to add your own ones on
That's if you are game

FOOTBALL IS RUBBISH

Football is rubbish
I don't care what you say
I'm not the slightest bit interested
Watching them play
I don't care if its England
I think that's it lame
No matter how much you tell me
It's the beautiful game
90 minutes of boredom
It's a nightmare for me
I don't give a stuff
If it was a penalty
Overpaid bloody ponces
Who can't take a hit
Rolling around like they're dying
Get up you soft tit
I'm sure the ref is a wanker
And bent and blind yes indeed
But give the amateur dramatics a rest
You make my heart bleed
And don't try to tell me
It's your country have pride
I'm not interested at all
I'll watch the other side
Last time I gave a toss
It'll come as no surprise
Was many many years ago
Watching Gary Lineker's thighs
I prefer things a bit rougher
And don't start with those thoughts
But I'll save my attentions
For real contact sports

CRAP BISCUITS

Today I tried a wagon wheel
Their new 'epic' orange flavour
But let me tell you honestly
It's a taste I didn't savour
I think the little orangey bit
Is made from toxic waste
At the very least invented by
Someone lacking a sense of taste
But its not the only crappy treat
I've come across oh no
There's lots of sad little biscuits
That frankly, well they blow
Take rich tea for starters
In fact just take them away
They really are the perfect thing
To spoil your cuppa and your day
They melt after a second
They leave nasty scum in your tea
Just because they completely lack
Structural integrity
And let's not forget the bourbon biscuit
You think chocolate ooh that's fun
But it tastes like shit
Covered in sugary grit
So you can stick them up your bum!
Yes biscuit companies
You have a lot to learn
From the digestive or hobnob
Give me a proper sturdy biscuit
That can stand up to the job
They're properly absorbent
And you can't eat more than three
The perfect accompaniment
For a cup of Yorkshire tea

HIDE THE BODY

Can anyone help me dispose of
A large item of waste?
It has to be very cleanly done
So they can't build a case
Its too big for me to do alone
And we have to do it quick
Cos its smelling pretty ripe now
Its starting to make me feel sick
I put him...it...in a bin bag
But they're too thin and started to rip
Cos they're the cheap ones from home bargains
Too see through for the tip
I tried to put it in the boot
But was overwhelmed by the pong
And I couldn't fit in lengthways
As its almost 6 feet long
I've dragged it down the garden
Thought I could leave it in the woods
Cos people dump all sorts in there
Body parts and household goods
I did try making it smaller
To reduce the effort and the strife
But all that I could find to cut
Was the little vegetable knife
I suppose that we could burn it
Not the worst idea that
But it may attract attention
The strong aroma of bacon fat
So come on give a girl a hand
It could be quite a laugh
If you're feeling quite creative
We could try an acid bath
Don't leave me here all desperate
My rubbish has nowhere to go
And I don't have the DIY skills
To lay a patio

ABOUT THE AUTHOR

Laura J Booker is a wife, mother, and obedient servant to her two cats. Born and bred in South Yorkshire Laura says it as it is, she began writing poetry during the first covid lockdown as a way to deal with the stress and find humour in those strange times, she continues to find strange things everywhere.